Conversations With The Little Girl Within

A Journey of Forgiveness, Healing, and Liberation from Unresolved Childhood Issues

Conversations With The Little Girl Within

A Journey of Forgiveness, Healing, and Liberation
from Unresolved Childhood Issues

Shirley Williams

Conversations With The Little Girl Within
Published by Purposely Created Publishing Group™

Copyright © 2017 Shirley Williams

All rights reserved.

No part of this book may be reproduced, distributed or transmitted in any form by any means, graphics, electronics, or mechanical, including photocopy, recording, taping, or by any information storage or retrieval system, without permission in writing from the publisher, except in the case of reprints in the context of reviews, quotes, or references.

Unless otherwise indicated, scripture quotations are from the Holy Bible, King James Version. All rights reserved.

Scriptures marked NIV are taken from the New International Version®. Copyright © 1973, 1978, 1984, 2011 by Biblica, Inc.™. All rights reserved.

Printed in the United States of America

ISBN: 978-1-947054-19-6

Special discounts are available on bulk quantity purchases by book clubs, associations and special interest groups. For details email: sales@publishyourgift.com or call (888) 949-6228.
For information logon to: www.PublishYourGift.com

This book is dedicated to our fathers and mothers, their fathers and mothers, their fathers and mothers, and the ancestral families who suffered in silence yet persevered in the midst of tremendous adversarial tests of their humanity in order for us to become empowered to break the cycle of generational afflictions.

CONTENTS

Prelude ix
Introduction 1

Chapter 1: Better Than Average 9
Chapter 2: The Eerie Confession 13
Chapter 3: Bizarre Occurrences 23
Chapter 4: Inquiring Minds Should Inquire 31
Chapter 5: Escaping My Reality 43
Chapter 6: Everything Makes Sense at Some Point ... 59
Chapter 7: Vitalized, No Longer a Victim 67
Chapter 8: The ABCs You Didn't Learn in School 73
Chapter 9: Revelations 83
Chapter 10: Conversations with the Little
Girl Within 93

Conclusion 111
Acknowledgments 115
About the Author 117
References 119
Resources and Other Information 121

PRELUDE

Everyone deserves a life that is filled with love, respect, and hope, and such a world can exist only if the wounded child that is still suffering inside gets treated.
—Dr. Laura Berman

At church, I met a woman, Ms. Ashburn, who happened to be a Reiki practitioner. We had similar interests and quickly became friends. When she learned I'd never experienced a Reiki session, she offered to give me a free session, so I took her up on it.

After the initial session, I realized Reiki could aid me in dealing with the stress from the personal issues I was struggling with. It was nice to have someone to talk with who understood spiritual living principles. I viewed the session as a means of enlightenment in my quest to understand the spiritual intricacies of life as it pertained to my evolution.

I followed that session up with another and began to respect and trust Ms. Ashburn's gift. As a student of the Universe who was ready to learn, I recognized that she was the teacher who presented the lesson I needed to learn at that time.

Reiki is a Japanese technique for stress reduction and relaxation, and it also promotes healing. It is administered by "laying on hands" and is based on the idea that an unseen "life force energy" flows through us and is what causes us to be alive.

The word Reiki is made up of two Japanese words: Rei, which means "God's Wisdom" or "the Higher Power," and Ki, which is "life force energy." So Reiki is actually "spiritually guided life force energy."

At the time I scheduled my next Reiki session with Ms. Ashburn, I was recovering from a violent situation, in addition to dealing with the pressures of starting a new job. The stress from the culmination of events of the previous few weeks was almost unbearable and had taken a serious toll on my health, landing me in the emergency room twice in one week. The scheduled Reiki session couldn't have arrived soon enough.

When the time came for the session, I lay on the table more relaxed than I'd been in almost three weeks. I could feel my body slowly begin to release the tense position it had assumed weeks earlier and I began to silently sing the words of one of my favorite songs.

As with most sessions, as Ms. Ashburn passed her hands over my body, I paid attention to the vibrations, feelings, and other sensations that occurred in my body. During this particular session, the sensations were stronger than usual in the areas of the third and fourth chakras. As Ms. Ashburn walked around the table doing the hands-off technique, I felt a sensation as though something heavy was still hovering over those regions.

The third chakra, the solar plexus chakra, is located around the upper abdomen in the stomach area and deals with the emotional issues of self-worth, self-confidence, and self-esteem. The fourth chakra, the heart chakra, is located in the center of the chest just above the heart and deals with the emotional issues of love, joy, and inner peace.

Generally, after a session, Ms. Ashburn and I would discuss and evaluate what we both sensed during the session. As I explained the strong sensations that seemed to be hovering around those chakras, she responded that she was getting goose bumps hearing that. She informed me that as she was concentrating on those specific regions, she had a very clear image of a little girl, possibly around the age of six or seven.

When I heard her say the words "little girl," a rush of emotions overwhelmed me, and I began to cry. I thought back to when I'd first started writing my book, which was about a completely different topic. I had written several chapters, and somehow it didn't feel quite like the book I was supposed to write. I knew I wanted to write about the subject and even had a title for that book, but it didn't seem to flow. I felt as if there was something else that needed to be expressed, but I couldn't figure out what that was.

I decided to take a break from writing that book in order to seek further clarification and guidance from the Source of Life. The first query I posed to the

Universe was, "What am I supposed to write about then?" Secondly, I conceded, "I'm just a yielded vessel for God to use." I then asked the Higher Power to reveal the direction the book should go. I released the concern, knowing the answer would be revealed at the right time.

Weeks later, during my morning journaling session, as I pondered the substance of the book, I heard the words "little girl" followed by "deal with your unresolved childhood issues." That was a surprise to me. As far as I knew, I didn't have any unresolved childhood issues. I had forgiven my mom many years earlier and thought I'd made peace with the past. I ruminated on those two phrases for some time, trying to get a clearer understanding of what the phrases meant. So when Ms. Ashburn mentioned the words "little girl" during our Reiki session, I knew immediately it had something to do with my book.

I listened intently as Ms. Ashburn described this child twirling and swinging around and around while moving up and down through the atmosphere, whimsically swinging her arms about in a joyous motion. Ms. Ashburn said that every time this child floated up in the air, as she came back down, she brought positive energy with her. She said that the little girl said she is happy now.

Tears began to flow again as I listened to Ms. Ashburn talk about how happy this child seemed and how much she wanted me to know that she loved me. She also mentioned that the child wanted me to know that "it's okay, we got this." She repeated, "We got this," almost apologetically, and stated that she "doesn't generally use language like that" and hoped I wasn't offended by what she said.

Ms. Ashburn continued talking, and the way she described the child floating through the air twirling ribbons reminded me of one of my fondest memories in grade school. I was in the first or second grade, and the class was on the playground participating in a collective Maypole dance. The colorful ribbons floating in the air as we twirled about looping over and under them, singing and dancing to the Maypole song, mesmerized me.

At the end of our session, Ms. Ashburn suggested that I consider talking to the little girl to see what other messages she had for me. I politely agreed to do so, although I wasn't in complete agreement. My mind filled with thoughts of contacting the dead from beyond the grave and all that spooky stuff. But I filed it away in my mind, certain that if it was relevant for the book then it seemed like a logical step.

On my drive home, a flood of questions raced through my mind. As I attempted to connect the dots, it became evident that the focus of the book would be unresolved childhood issues. I made a mental note to meditate on whether I still had unresolved issues from my childhood in order to get clarity.

I began to wonder if I had masked some anger that, after all these years, still lingered in the depth of my being. There were times over the years I'd hear that old record playing in my head, my mother's voice telling me "you'll never be anything," or "shut up, nobody wants to hear what you have to say." I often wondered if I had been unconsciously self-sabotaging just to prove her right. I wondered if that was the reason I felt stuck, unable to move beyond a certain point in my life. Talk about a slap in the face of reality—but why now?

I had already gone through the rituals of forgiving my mother. I was free from the burden of disappointments and hurts from my childhood. Was the forgiveness just that—a ritual from the head and not genuinely from my heart? I assumed the purpose of forgiveness was to come to the point of accepting the traumatic events that happened and moving on with my life. I suddenly realized there had to be more depth to the issue of forgiveness and I had only tapped the surface.

Maybe there was some residual baggage buried deep in my subconscious that needed to be uncovered. I had to be receptive to the notion that maybe I hadn't forgiven my mom after all. Obviously, it was time for me to deal with any unresolved issues once and for all.

Thank you, Little Shirley, for showing up and letting me know that you are happy and that "we got this." It strengthens my hope! People will want to hear what we have to say.

INTRODUCTION

*Broken adults are broken children who need
healing in order to be set free.*

Most children are not adequately equipped to deal with conflicts in the home environment or other traumatic incidents that happen to them, so they develop internal methods to cope with the situation in order to survive and maintain some semblance of sanity as they move forward in life. As the wounded child moves forward into adulthood, he or she will develop ways to specifically cope with their unspeakable hurts and pain from childhood.

Signs of Unresolved Trauma[1]

If you're reading this book, you are probably one of the millions of people dealing with the painful reality of unresolved adverse childhood experiences. According to Promises Malibu Vista's website, some of the signs indicating that unresolved trauma is present are:

- Risk-taking behavior
- Desire to self-medicate with alcohol or drugs
- Chronic or recurring depression or feelings of despair

- Emotional constriction/lack of affect and spontaneity
- Drive to re-create painful emotional dynamics
- Loss of ability to modulate emotion
- Inability to take in support
- Psychosomatic symptoms
- Hypervigilance

Addiction, depression, anxiety disorders, post-traumatic stress disorders, and even certain chronic diseases such as heart disease and type 2 diabetes are found more frequently in people who had a traumatic childhood, and for these reasons alone, the issue of working through grief and trauma should be taken very seriously.

Many people suppress painful memories and emotions—sometimes for decades—or are simply unwilling to look at the source of the painful emotions they feel, the disconnection they experience from others and from their lives, and the problems they continually encounter in relationships. Sorting through one's past trauma is key to healing these issues and is crucial to one's health and potentially to the health of one's children.

Although the past cannot be changed, one's reactions to it, both conscious and unconscious can be. Bringing unconscious thought patterns to the surface of awareness and committing to heal may be a life-saving step; it can certainly be a life-changing one. Working with a good therapist, finding a support group, reaching out to people who share a similar history, and reading supportive books about how to cope with the past and create a healthier today are some ways people are healing from their past every day. Even someone with a tragic past can learn to trust others, create a healthy, stable relationship, and approach their world from a state of calm, inner peace, and knowing. These gifts are not merely for those who are lucky or who live charmed existences; they are the reality of anyone willing to reach inside themselves with compassion and work to heal the past.

The Stubborn Child

Most parents know what it's like to have a stubborn child who decides to have a temper tantrum because they can't get their way, and the tantrum usually occurs in a public place. The child will get angry, stomp their feet, fold their arms across their chest, or stop in their tracks, refusing to move further.

The parent is left standing there, bewildered, looking at this three- or four-year-old child and begging him or her to "come on, honey." Only, the child just stands there staring at the parent and pouting. The child will not budge until the parent eventually walks over to him or her, takes the child by the hand, and forces him or her to come along.

Your unresolved issues are like this stubborn child. Until you force yourself to look at your issues squarely in the face and challenge yourself to address them, you'll continue to be haunted by your adverse childhood experiences and continue acting out in ways that may be detrimental to your physical and emotional well-being.

As Time Goes By

Often, adults have many issues that stem from their childhood that impede their ability to mature beyond a certain point, even well into their adult life. Unfortunately, time does not wait for us to catch up; it continues to move forward as we continue to mature physically. Psychologically, we're still a child having temper tantrums, but now, as adults, we're acting out in irresponsible ways.

There are billions of children disguised as adults, who live recklessly because of unresolved childhood issues. Adults often don't realize how these issues have stymied their satisfaction in life already, as well as their relevance to their responses to certain situations that arise throughout their lives.

Parents should comprehend how their actions in the home environment reflect back on the lives of the children they're raising. Children learn what they live. If you're a broken adult child who was abused in any way during your childhood, you have the propensity to become an abuser as an adult, unless you heal at some point. To the parent who is reading this book, realize that when you break a child's spirit at a young age, you've essentially caused that child to remain stuck at that point in time until healing occurs.

Throughout my life, I've encountered hundreds of adults who are well into life and talk freely about their traumatic issues, yet they don't attribute the negative effects appropriately to their current relationships and lifestyle. They've relived and retold their stories thousands of times and with the same emotional intensity. Many have resigned to living a less-than-fulfilling life because they remain stuck emotionally at the age of their traumatic childhood experience. Sometimes, the negative effects of traumatic issues manifest in ways such as:

- Lacking self-discipline to complete a task or project, especially when it's for your own fulfillment
- Dwelling in resentment when things don't go your way
- Feeling powerless and pleasing others to gain some sense of control
- Perceiving yourself like a victim in any way or blaming others for your emotional states
- Expecting people to do what you need or want, as if they owe you something
- Making excuses or justifying yourself, as if you owe them something[2]

I was a little girl with so much talent and ambition for my life, but I dared not to speak up, manifest, or believe in myself until well into my adult life. I was a little girl stuck in an adult woman's body. I wasn't aware of being a slave to my little girl's antics until I took the steps necessary to restore my life in an attempt to finally let go of the emotional baggage that I carried throughout my life.

My journey of recovering from my wounded childhood was multifaceted. I buried the painful memories so deep that it took over twenty years for them to resurface. When they did, there were many nights of uncontrollable sobbing, questioning God, anger, hatred, and resentment toward my mother. It took a few years to work on forgiveness, and when I thought I had absolved my mother, years later I discovered I needed to do more work.

After attending a weekend workshop to help me transform self-limiting beliefs, I learned just how deep my dislike was for my mother. I discovered that subconsciously I was still holding on to resentment and I was surprised to learn that I did not love her. After successfully completing the workshop, I am stronger emotionally, and now, instead of hearing the old records playing from the past, I am rewriting the script for my life and infusing it with empowering, well-formed, and compelling goal statements. Those painful memories have been resolved, and I am living in greater peace and happiness as a result!

On the conscious level, you can lie to yourself, but the subconscious level is the storehouse of everything, including the skeletons in your closet that still haunt you. All of your secrets that only you and God know about are embedded in your subconscious mind. You can't deny the facts.

It is my intention for this book to provoke you to reflect on your life and recognize areas where you may be stuck—areas that could be the result of your unresolved childhood matter. I pray that by sharing my experience in this book, you will be enlightened about unresolved childhood issues and hopefully understand that continuing to suppress the issues can impact your adult life. I encourage you to face your fears.

It may be wise to seek professional assistance from a practitioner familiar with adverse childhood experiences (ACEs). In addition, on the spiritual level, I can testify that with the assistance of your Holy Helper, if you delve into the depths of your soul to seek answers to your queries, the Universe will provide the answers, the understanding, and the support you need to heal from your painful memories. It's time to set free the wounded child inside you from the bondage of the past, so you can live your authentic adult life.

Chapter 1
BETTER THAN AVERAGE

> *You are entitled to every good thing. Therefore expect nothing but good.*
> —Robert Collier, The Secret of the Ages

Before I started elementary school, I'd hear the older kids in the neighborhood talk about skipping grades in school. They were exceptionally smart, and advanced through school seemingly much faster than the average kids. I wanted to follow in their footsteps and was eager to be in school.

When my mother registered my older sister and me for elementary school, we had to take a placement test, and I scored higher on it. The principal wanted to place me in the first grade instead of kindergarten. I was excited about the thought of skipping a grade because that proved to me that I was indeed smart. I was determined in that moment that I was going to skip my way through school—when suddenly my daydreaming was interrupted when I heard my mother object. She firmly told the principal that my sister was older, so she should be in the first grade, and I was to go to kindergarten.

As I sat on the bench listening to her talking to the principal about me as if I wasn't even present, I felt a deep sense of sadness. I wondered why she would do that and thought it was a mean thing to do. It was as though my achievement didn't matter. I felt I had earned the privilege of skipping a grade and my mother was holding me back from progressing. I was disheartened, and needless to say, I hated kindergarten after that. Maybe that was when I started to subconsciously dislike my mother.

I was an adventurous and curious child. Being so far ahead in my thinking as a young child, I was very inquisitive about life and how I fit into the grand scheme of it. I was a blank slate and eager to learn, though there didn't seem to be anyone to guide me on this journey of knowledge. All I longed for was for someone to take an interest in me, and teach me how to exist in this world. I was full of ideas for my future and I had no idea how any of them were going to happen. Nevertheless, I expected to do great things. Because of my curiosity about life, I realized very early on that there was more to my life than just my biological family.

I liked exploring new places and learning new things, and I loved being outdoors in nature. I looked forward to waking up and experiencing what the world had to offer for the day. Before I would go outside to play, I often wondered, what adventures could I have? What new things could I create? What new thing was there to learn about life?

Chapter 2

THE EERIE CONFESSION

> *Be careful what you say. You can say something hurtful in ten seconds, but ten years later, the wounds are still there.*
>
> —Joel Olsteen

Everyone in the family was sitting around the table during dinner, my sisters and brother and both parents. I was about six or seven years old at the time. It was a warm summer evening, and both my parents were in a good mood. Once the kitchen was clean, they sat back down at the table to play a game of cards. It was rare to see them laughing and having a good time with each other.

My siblings left the kitchen and went to their rooms. I wanted to join in the fun, so I asked Father what they were playing and if I could play as well. He responded they were playing a game called Trunk and he allowed me to join in. As my father proceeded to explain the game, I noticed Mother get up from the table to pour herself a drink of Seagram's 7 whiskey and sit back down.

What I didn't realize was that by asking to join in the game, I had interrupted a rare moment they were sharing. It was one of the first times in a long time they were getting along. I had diverted my father's attention away from my mother, and like most insecure women, even though I was her child, she felt I was a menace in that moment. She was no longer the object of his attention.

My mother was drinking rather heavily and she got up from the table to fix herself another drink. My sister and brother came back into the kitchen and asked to join the game as well.

After about a half hour or so of playing cards, my mother began to talk about her life growing up in the South. Then she started talking about how she never thought about having children. She said that after she had my older siblings and found out she was pregnant again that she tried to abort the baby—me. She went into detail about how some of her girlfriends told her what to do to "get rid of it." One method was to use a clothes hanger to scrape "it" out and then douche with a bottle of Coca Cola. She followed that procedure with drinking a bottle of hot sauce. She complained that nothing she tried had worked.

Although I didn't fully understand all that she said, I sensed her disdain by the sharp and hateful tone of her voice as she told her tale. It sent chills through my young body, and I stiffened from the coldness of her words. I listened in horror as that woman described how she had tried to kill me. As she talked, she stared out into space without blinking, as if she were reliving the event. My father was appalled and told her several times to "shut up," but she kept on blabbing. I knew in that moment that I hated her for what she had just revealed.

To add insult to injury, my siblings thought the tale was amusing and began laughing and mocking me, saying, "Mommy didn't want you." I finally ran out of the kitchen and into my bedroom, sobbing.

My father came into the room shortly thereafter to console me. I was inconsolable and unable to move from the fetal position my body assumed. He stood by the bed and said, "Shirley, you know how your mama is when she's drinking. You know she didn't mean what she said."

He stood there a moment, possibly waiting for me to respond, and then walked out of the room. It didn't matter to me what he said about her—she had said she didn't want me and tried to kill me. It hurt so deeply, nothing my father said could take away that pain.

The Impact of that Confession

That night, as I finally started dozing off to sleep, I felt as if I was drifting through life. It seemed surreal, almost as if I were being dragged through a scary place I didn't want to be in, like being in a parallel universe and being an observer of my life.

It was a Friday evening when my mother made that confession. The next day, Saturday, was the day we did household chores. I lay in bed, afraid to get up. I did not want to face my mother because I did not know how to react to her after what she had disclosed. She was a stranger to me. I wondered who that woman really was. How could she say such a horrible thing? I felt no love for her, only hatred for what she had said, which was proof that she didn't love me.

I couldn't stop thinking about what she had confessed or hearing my siblings laughing at me. All I wanted to do when I got out of bed was to get out of the apartment as quickly as possible and never come back.

As I lay in bed, I listened for my father's voice. I didn't hear him, so I assumed he had left the apartment pretty early and wondered how he felt about what she had said. I so badly wanted him to hit her. But they didn't fight over it, and I felt somewhat betrayed by him. I felt he sort of defended her by excusing what she said because she was drunk. I wanted him to stand up for me—just telling her to shut up wasn't good enough. He let me down. I think he was afraid of her.

I smelled bacon and sage sausages cooking in the kitchen, and I heard pans clattering on the stove as my mother prepared breakfast. Saturday morning breakfast was my favorite day of the week to eat breakfast, but I wasn't hungry that morning.

I finally got out of bed, got dressed, and meandered around the bedroom. I shared the bedroom with my sister. She was already up and in the living room watching Saturday morning cartoons. I quietly wandered down the hallway, wishing in that moment that I were invisible. I meandered into the kitchen to see what she had cooked. I was surprised to see that she had made biscuits with breakfast. I liked biscuits. I don't know if that was her way of expressing remorse because she didn't make them often.

She was facing the stove, her back turned so she couldn't see me, so I quickly turned and went into the living room to watch cartoons. I had hoped watching television would take my mind off hearing her voice in my head speaking those awful things about me. I was reticent, yet I still felt some kind of way. I was wounded and felt very sad, perplexed, and awkward.

I was glad that after she cooked breakfast, she did what she always did: retreat into her bedroom where she typically stayed in bed watching television and sleeping.

I recognized that the atmosphere was highly tense in the apartment. We didn't speak to each other much that morning other than when she assigned me my chores. That was probably one of the rare times I was glad to have other siblings, so she had other children to divert her attention from me.

What was there to say, anyway? I don't know that anything she said could have healed that wound. You can't put the words back in your mouth after you've released them. I felt very somber, I was wounded by her hurtful words, and I was humiliated. None of my siblings spoke about the incident; no one asked me how I felt. I couldn't wait to finish my chores and get out of the house and to the beach, my safe haven.

In hindsight, I believe the sensitive nature of the confession and possibly her embarrassment afterwards helped me to remain calm when I wanted to scream and have a temper tantrum. Since I didn't know what to expect from her, I didn't want to say or do anything that would provoke her. I thought she might find any little reason to beat me if I did. I was frightened to be in her presence, and I tried to act as normally as possible, making no attempts to talk to her.

Once my sister and I finished our chores, we left the apartment. As soon as we walked outside and far enough away from the apartment, I started crying and shouted, "I hate her guts!" My astonished sister grabbed me by both arms, turned me toward her, gently shook me, and said, "Don't you ever say that again about Mommy. The Bible says you're supposed to honor your mother. Don't you know that God will punish you for saying that? You could walk outside and a bus will run you over for saying something like that." And she was serious too.

I couldn't wait to get to the beach. That was the one place I loved to go to ponder my queries to the Universe and try to understand the logic of this thing called life.

I'd sit for hours watching the waves roll in and roll out from the shore. It was therapeutic to me, as if the waves were washing away all my sorrows. That was my outlet. I didn't have to talk to anyone or listen to anyone tell me what to do. I'd just sit on the sand or on the benches, and many times I would just stroll along the beach for hours.

When I finally arrived at the beach, I trudged through the sand and down to the shoreline. I screamed, "I hate you!" and fell down on my knees in the sand, crying. It felt good to release the pent up anger.

Several hours later, after much reflection, I realized that there must be a reason for me being alive. Otherwise, why hadn't I died when she did all the horrible things she described?

I didn't consciously think about there being "a purpose for my life" the way we talk about it today. I just thought I was alive for a reason, and I felt a little special and proud that I had survived. That thought made me feel a little better.

To some extent, a part of me didn't want to believe my mother's story. I thought maybe she was just being vicious and mean because I interrupted the moment that she was having with my dad. Maybe her saying those hurtful things was her way of getting back at me. And even though it had a strong effect on me, I may have diminished it on some level as her just being her hateful self, like my dad had said. I also felt that, for her, being a mother must have been burdensome. I decided I did not want to have children.

When I left the beach that Saturday after her confession, I left that burden there and buried it so deep inside of me, vowing never to think about it again.

Maybe my mother couldn't kill me physically, but it seemed as though she was good at killing any aspirations I began to develop for myself. Once again, a dream was interrupted. In the sixth grade, I was offered the opportunity to go to a magnet school for the arts in the city.

My sixth grade teacher had invited one of her colleagues to speak to the class, and afterwards, she introduced the woman to me. My teacher mentioned that I'd already written a full play, was an excellent writer, and was talented in fashion design. Her colleague asked to view my writings and my drawings, so I retrieved my books and showed them to her. Before the woman left, she asked to take my sketches and my notebook with her and said she'd "be in touch".

A few weeks later, she contacted my mother to talk to her about me attending the magnet school. I stood in the hallway in our apartment, listening to my mother talk with the woman over the phone. I was dismayed when I heard my mother tell the woman that "she didn't have money to send me to school in the city," and she "did not want me traveling alone all the way to the city to go to some school."

I was so very disappointed that I would not be attending the magnet school. If other people felt I had talent, I wondered, why was she so against me going? I did not know what I did to make her hate me so much. In that moment, I felt my zest for life begin to diminish, and hopelessness and anger took its place.

This time, I wasn't a five-year-old child sitting on a bench in the principal's office listening to her talk about me as if I wasn't present. After my mother rudely hung up on the woman, I hastily approached her in my anger, demanding to know why I couldn't go to that school. She looked at me, put her hands on her hips, and said in a loud and stern voice, "You're not going to some damn school in the city. You're going to keep your ass right here and go to the school up the street just like everyone else."

I had learned that when she put her hands on her hips, the next thing would be the slap upside the head that you didn't see coming. I backed away and stormed out of the house and headed to the beach.

After that, I stopped writing and designing. Needless to say, I hated junior high and thus began acting out in school. My junior high school years were very tumultuous. All I wanted was to finish school so I could get away from her as fast as possible.

Chapter 3

BIZARRE OCCURRENCES

> To live by grace means to acknowledge my whole life story, the light side and the dark. In admitting my shadow side, I learn who I am and what God's grace means.
> —Brennan Manning, *The Ragamuffin Gospel*

During my later elementary school years up to about my second year in junior high school, I had a series of bizarre and uncanny experiences. I often felt as if "something" was following me around. It seemed to be either a shadowy presence that frightened me or some invisible force that protected me.

My favorite places to hang out during my adolescent years were the public library and the beach. I particularly liked story hours at the library even though I was much older than most of the children.

One day, I was at the library for a reading of Charlotte's Web. I sat on the floor in the library with the other children, listening to the librarian read some of the story to us. She held us spellbound as she read the words, shifting her tones to emphasize the voices of the different characters. I enjoyed listening to the story, and before I knew, the hour had gone by.

Once the reading was over, I quickly ran to the bookshelf to get a copy of the book so I could read the rest of the story. I finished reading it just as the library was about to close. I dreaded going home after leaving the library because it was late and I knew Mother would have something to scream at me about when I arrived. I decided not to take my regular route and headed toward the boardwalk to walk the few miles home along the beach.

As I strolled along the boardwalk, still thinking about story hour, I experienced a warm sensation that enveloped my entire body. It felt as if a pair of arms had embraced me, and it was such a loving and peaceful impression. In that second, the earth plane seemed to disappear, and I felt as if I were floating. I seemed to be caught up in a state of heavenly bliss or some sort of out-of-body experience.

I had no idea how long I'd been in that state, but the next thing I knew, I was standing in front of my apartment door, lightheaded and boggled, trying to compose myself before going inside. That was the first experience I had with what I refer to as "the Sensation."

Throughout the next five or so years, it seemed that whenever I found myself in a dangerous situation, "the Sensation" or possibly my guardian angel, would embrace me and bring me to safety. What was interesting about "the Sensation" was that when I was caught up in it, all of my physical senses appeared to be muted. I wasn't consciously aware of my surroundings or in control of my intellect until I was out of danger. I began to look at life differently and had so many questions but still no one to ask.

Afterwards, when I would snap out of the trance-like state, I'd realize something bizarre had just happened. Although it frightened me and I didn't understand what had happened, initially, I did not try to analyze these moments. I would run away from the situation as fast as I could and never speak of the incidents to anyone. After all, who would believe me, anyway? Heck, I couldn't even logically comprehend "It" enough to explain to anyone.

I tried to be as normal as possible after the bizarre happenings occurred. If anyone knew, they'd think I was crazy. There were already a few people in the neighborhood who "were crazy." It seemed like anyone who acted weirdly or spoke about subjects most people weren't familiar with was classified as crazy, and we were told to "watch out for them." Granted, one or two of them did walk around seeing things that weren't there—for instance, one neighbor was sitting in our apartment and staring out the window when she asked my mother "if she saw that train crossing the bay."

My mother politely told her, "I think it's time for you to go home now."

Deep down inside, I felt there was something different about me. I recognized it more and more and couldn't quite put my finger on it, but it made me feel like an alien. There was a deep awareness of a spiritual realm that some part of me seemed connected to. I began to look at life differently and had so many questions but still no one to ask. No one around me was as curious about life as I was. They didn't talk about life beyond our present reality; heck, they didn't even talk about future plans.

The Elevator

In the projects I grew up in, the elevators went out of order often. There were times you could open the door and the elevator would be on another floor. One summer evening, when I was about ten or eleven years of age, I was visiting with a friend at her apartment a few buildings over from where I lived. She lived on the sixth floor with her family. It was dinnertime, so I left to go home just as her family was preparing to sit down to eat.

On this particular day, instead of taking the stairs, I chose to take the elevator. I walked over to the elevator, pressed the button, and waited a few seconds. I heard the ding sound that alerted me of the elevator's arrival. I impulsively pulled opened the door, took a step in, and heard what seemed like an echo of the sound of the door closing behind me.

Instantly, everything went pitch black, and I was overcome by "the Sensation." I felt as if I had stepped onto something that held me up, and I felt a movement that shifted up slightly and then traveled backwards. The next thing I knew, I was back on solid ground, stumbling against the wall as if I had been gently tossed backwards.

Even though I sensed my movements, I wasn't aware of what was happening until after I snapped out of the trance-like state. It took a moment for me to collect myself, and as I staggered to get up, I noticed my heart was pounding faster than it ever had before. I could hardly breathe.

I tried to figure out what had just happened and realized that I'd walked into the elevator shaft. Stunned, I stood up and said, "Oh shit." I ran to the stairwell, jumped down the stairs a flight at a time, and didn't stop running until I got home.

When I rushed into the apartment, my mother was in the kitchen. I must have frightened her because she hollered, "What the hell you come barging in the door like that for, you crazy or something?"

I said "no" as I rushed into the bathroom, closed the door, and sat on the bathtub crying. I was terrified and shaken. I knew then that whatever had happened, "something" had kept me from falling down that elevator shaft.

I'd heard the horror stories of kids being killed by falling down elevator shafts. I'd even seen remnants of the human remains of someone I knew who was crushed when he fell between floors while riding on top of an elevator. All I could think was that could have been me.

I kept replaying what I remembered over and over, hearing the ding sound of the elevator arriving and seeing the light inside it. As hard as I tried, I couldn't figure out what had prevented me from falling; it was unbelievable and it frightened the heck out of me. There was no plausible explanation for this bizarre event, which seemed to be a supernatural experience. I was furious and bewildered, wondering if I was going crazy. I became hysterical and stumbled backwards into the bathtub, hitting my head on the faucet. The shower curtain and rod fell down on top of me.

My mother came rushing into the bathroom and asked, "What the hell is wrong with you? What are you doing in here?"

I was crying and said I didn't feel well, that I had fallen into the bathtub.

She told me to pick up the shower curtains and take my ass to bed.

I did as ordered.

When I woke up the next morning, I had the worst headache of my life. I went into the kitchen and told my mother I didn't feel well. She replied that I wasn't staying home from school. My head was pounding. I felt like I was going to throw up. Without eating breakfast, I dressed, gathered my schoolbooks, and headed out the door.

As soon as I stepped outside the apartment, the queasiness returned. By the time I reached the stairwell, I began throwing up—a lot. Feeling weak, I slid down the wall and sat on the floor crying. My head was pounding, and by then it seemed just to be on one side. All I could see was a big black dot, and I felt a tingling sensation in my hands. The tingling moved from one finger to the next. It was terrifying. I had no idea what was happening to me. I felt as if I were living a nightmare.

I'm not sure how long I sat there on the floor, but the janitor who was assigned to our building arrived to clean and saw me sitting there. He asked if I was okay, and I mumbled that I didn't feel well.

He asked if my mother knew I was outside. After I mumbled no, he rushed to knock on the apartment door to alert my mother that I was sick in the hallway. I could hear her saying, "Ain't nothing wrong with Shirley, she just don't want to go to school today."

He told her that I'd thrown up in the hallway, and she yelled for me to "get my ass in the house."

He came back, helped me up, and took me back to the apartment.

That was the beginning of a series of migraine headaches I'd suffer from for many years to come. I never spoke of the elevator incident to anyone.

As I grew into adulthood, that "Sensation" evolved into the still, small voice of God that continues to guide and protect me.

Chapter 4
INQUIRING MINDS SHOULD INQUIRE

> *Each of us has to go back to our family experience, that childhood time and place and review what happened. Once we become conscious of our control drama, then we can focus on the higher truth of our family, the silver lining so to speak, that lies beyond the energy conflict. Once we find this truth, it can energize our lives, for this truth tells us who we are, the path we are on, what we are doing.*
> —James Redfield, *The Celestine Prophecy*

Whenever possible, inquire about your parent's history because how they were treated will most likely be reflected in how they treated and raised you. Learn the lessons from their upbringing. Our parents, too, were little children who grew up and lived out the messages they received from their childhood, whether good or bad. Little do we know that the disempowering messages we receive from childhood can dictate most of our adult beliefs; that is until we accept a new set of beliefs for our lives and rewrite the script.

My parents were born about a generation or two out of slavery. Neither of them had much of an education. Both were born in the South, and from the stories my father told about his life, it didn't seem like he had any schooling beyond elementary level. My mother did not talk very much about her life, but she may have completed high school at the most. Since neither of them were not education minded, they didn't encourage me to get an education beyond high school.

Daddy's Little Girl

I was a daddy's girl. He was my hero and the love of my life. To me, he epitomized love—love of self, family, and humankind in general. My dad didn't go to church, but was spiritual in his own way. He loved God and often referred to God as "The Master." Whenever he talked to me about "The Master," something about his countenance shifted. It was almost as if he were talking about a dear friend. Whoever The Master was, I loved Him too. Whatever could cause such deep devotion and sense of peace in my dad was also worthy of my attention and respect.

Dad wasn't a complainer by any means. He took his responsibilities seriously and did what he needed to do within the confines of the law to survive and provide for his family. I loved being with my dad and following him around whenever he went on his handyman jobs. My father did not have a car, so he would tote his red toolbox back and forth for miles up and down the neighborhood. He carried it so easily. I never thought about how heavy it might have been until I attempted to pick it up one day.

I took full advantage of any opportunity to spend time with him, and no matter where it took us, it was going to be an adventure. He was the local handyman, and anything someone needed repaired, he was the man to call. He would take little or no money for his services. He could fix washing machines and television sets, lay carpet, do electrical work, and take care of anything else that needed to be repaired, replaced, or rewired.

At times, he and I would roam the neighborhood scavenging for appliances and other electronic items that people discarded. If he didn't want to keep an item after he had repaired it, he'd often sell it or give it away to someone in need.

My dad genuinely cared for people, especially senior citizens and little children. He always looked out for the well-being of the elderly neighbors in the apartment buildings on both sides of the projects we lived in, as well as throughout the neighborhood.

I was so proud of him. To me, he was like a celebrity. Every place we went, people knew him, and he always took time to talk with them. When he introduced me to people as his daughter, that made me feel special and deepened my admiration for him all the more.

What's Her Story?

When my mother left the South, she never looked back. She wasn't a social woman or friendly the way my father was. She seemed to be somewhat of an unhappy person, and I often wondered through the years if she had regrets about her life. Maybe she felt guilt and shame about things she did in her life before she met and married my dad and had children. I wondered if she disliked me so much because I reminded her of someone from her past.

I think to a large extent she could have suffered from some form of depression. Raising children while trying to manage her personal and private sufferings had to be difficult. She put her energy into the role of functioning as a housewife and controlling her children. As she adapted to the role, she showed preference to my brother and sister, the children who appealed to her most. She even had pet names for them. She didn't take much interest in me, and as much as I vied for her attention, I remained the black sheep. I was the child she took her frustrations out on, but my father and older sister were not excluded from her wrath. My father too bore a lot of physical abuse from her. As I got older and learned more about life, I believe my mother unconsciously retaliated with violence against my dad because he was symbolic of all the men who had treated her badly from her past relationships. Those men may have abused her—she may have felt helpless and defenseless—so she conveniently wrapped up all that rage and projected it onto my dad.

The physical and verbal abuse from my mother was confusing growing up. I inherently surmised that a mother's role was to actively engage in her children's lives, to show love and concern for their well-being. Maybe watching the Cleavers on the television program Leave it to Beaver, or observing the relationships my friends had with their mothers, or even the way my aunt and cousins engaged with their children, shaped my idea of what a mother was supposed to be.

I read in the book The Celestine Prophecy that "in any family the child must first receive energy from the adults in his life." Usually, identifying with and integrating the energy of the same-sexed parent is accomplished easily. It's possible I received the masculine energy from my father but not my mother's feminine energy. I believe part of the reason it was difficult for me to relate to my mother, and to some extent, other women as I advanced in life, is because I didn't receive that feminine energy as a child. Since I couldn't identify with my mother, my identity, my sense of self, wasn't completely established during my formative years.

For most of my adolescent years, my mother was distant. She was an enigma to me and so apathetic. It seemed almost as if she were live-in hired help. One thing I did appreciate growing up was her home cooking. She was a very good southern cook and kept a clean house. In that sense, she upheld her motherly duties.

My mother was religious and always in church. She sang in the choir and was on the usher board. She made sure we went to church every Sunday, too. However, as a child, I wasn't impressed with church at all. I watched people I knew pretend to be saintly in church, while outside of church, they lived totally different lives. My mother was a good Christian woman in church on Sunday, but the rest of the week at home, when she wasn't performing her Sister So and So church roles, she could be one of the meanest people in the world.

Because I saw that most of the adults seemed to behave one way in church and another way at home, I surmised that going to church was something you had to do to "get through the Pearly Gates when you die."

The Worst Beating I Ever Endured

It was difficult to cope with the trauma of being mercilessly beaten with an ironing cord by my mother. On top of knowing that my mother had so much rage in her that she could beat me in such a savage manner, and usually over minor incidents, the horrible pain of the beatings was incomprehensible.

Each time my mother hit me, it stunned me, and I would hold my breath with each strike, trying not to feel the sting from the lashings. I would imagine being in an invisible box that protected me from the pain, and I'd peek out waiting for her to stop swinging. When she did and I saw her leave the room, the box would disappear. Then my whole body would begin to sting and throb in excruciating pain. All I was able to do was lie absolutely still, wait for the pain to subside, and then crawl into bed and cry myself to sleep.

My mother was a domestic worker and took pride in working for the Jewish families who provided her a meager wage for cleaning their apartments. One day during the summer of the end of my fifth-grade term, for whatever reason, my mother didn't go to her domestic job and wanted me to substitute for her.

After she finished her phone call to the woman, she summoned me into the kitchen and told me that I was going to Mrs. So and So's house to clean it. She instructed me how to clean the apartment, what areas to clean, where not to clean, and lastly, ordered me not to touch anything in the house. She warned, "The woman knows where every little thing belongs and will know if anything is out of order."

I looked at my mother rebelliously and asked, "Why do I have to go and not my older sibling?"

She immediately gave me that look, and I knew to shut up before I got knocked upside my head with the backhanded slap I never saw coming. She responded, "Because I told you to," in a tone of voice that implied if she had to say another word about it, I'd get that slap. She walked away into the back room to retrieve her purse to get bus fare for me.

Once outside, still angry and pouting, I decided to walk the seven or eight miles to the woman's apartment complex. She was expecting me, and when I arrived, she phoned my mother to let her know I'd made it.

I went through the apartment, cleaning and dusting as ordered, and began dusting a roll top desk in the foyer. Out of mere curiosity, I opened the desk and pulled open a small drawer to find several books of postage stamps. Even though I had no use for the stamps, I picked them up and stuck them in my back pocket. I knew I shouldn't have, but I was still angry about having to perform domestic work. I thought, "I'll show her, got me cleaning these white folks' place like I'm a slave."

Once I finished the work, about three hours later, I went to the bedroom to let Mrs. So and So know I'd finished the chores. She rose from the bed and thanked me for coming as she walked me to the front door. I stood there waiting for her to pay me, but she never did. Instead, she said, "I'll let your mother know how you did."

I didn't care because I wasn't ever going back there again. Did she think I was my mother's apprentice?

When I arrived home, my mother was in the kitchen. In a calm voice, which should have been a warning to me, she asked how it went. Before I could say anything, she slapped me across the face and began yelling, "Mrs. So and So called me upset because a book of stamps is missing from the desk and she wondered if you had seen them! I told you not to touch anything in that house. I worked for that woman for ten years and nothing ever came up missing and you go there one time and take some got damn stamps. Give me them damn stamps."

As I reached into my pocket to get them, she pulled a chair from the kitchen table and retrieved the ironing cord. I dropped the stamps and immediately ran into the bedroom and scooted under the bed to get away from her. In a rage, she began dismantling the bed. The bed fell on top of me, and I rolled out from under it. She swung at me, striking me twice before the ironing cord flung from her hand. She began kicking at me and then started stomping me. As I screamed and cried that I was sorry, she continued stomping me in the stomach. After the third or fourth stomp, the contents of my bowels spilled out. Just as she was about to stomp me again, I mustered up enough strength to say, "You're going to kill me." At that point, she looked down at me. Perspiring and out of breath, she turned and walked out of the room.

I don't know how long I was on the floor unable to move. I couldn't feel anything or think. My mind felt numb, and I could hardly breathe. Each breath was painful and shallow. It was as though I had floated out of my body and was hovering over it. I looked back and saw something that appeared to be a dark glob on the floor. I was in a dreamlike state and then saw my sister, as if in slow motion, reaching out her hand. She was crying and calling my name, telling me to get up as she tried to help me off the floor.

She managed to get me on the bed, and I looked back and saw her cleaning the mess up off the floor. I kept thinking, I'm so sorry, over and over, as if it was a prayer of repentance, and with a deep sense of sorrow, I fell asleep.

I was awakened by my mother's voice yelling at me to get my ass up and go back to that woman's house to return the stamps. I was in so much pain and so disoriented, I could hardly move, but I managed to get to the bathroom to wash up and change clothes. I walked into the kitchen without saying a word, picked up the stamps from the table, and walked out the door. My mother never turned to look at me, nor did she say a word as I walked out.

I walked to the bus stop to catch the bus back to Mrs. So and So's apartment. I hated my mother even more and didn't ever want to see her again. I wondered why she just didn't go ahead and kill me; after all, she didn't want me anyway.

When I arrived at the lady's apartment, I reluctantly knocked on the door. She opened it, and when she saw me, her mouth dropped open. But before she could say anything, I threw the stamps on the floor, turned, and walked away without saying a word. I was about ten years old, and that was the first time I ran away from home.

The landmark adverse childhood experiences (ACE) study by the Centers for Disease Control and Prevention (CDC, 2014) examined a mainstream, insured adult US population, and demonstrated that over 60 percent had experienced childhood trauma, with 16 percent reporting complex trauma (multiple types of abuse, severe abuse, or abuse over a long period). Even higher rates of physical and emotional child abuse were found in a recent study of a more diverse US sample.[4]

Chapter 5
ESCAPING MY REALITY

> *Your life does not get better by chance, it gets better by change.*
> —Jim Rohn

Every time I'd run away from home, I'd explore rooftops, elevator rooms, mechanical rooms, and janitorial closets throughout the community in search of places to spend the night. When I discovered someplace I felt was safe, that's where I'd crash for the night.

During these times of solitude, often I'd cry myself to sleep. There were many times, though, when I'd sit awake until two or three o'clock in the morning, thinking about my life and imagining what it would be like if I were a sibling to one of my friends or cousins who had parents who cared about them.

Sometimes I'd get up early and walk around the neighborhood until what I thought was a decent hour, and then go to my best friend's house early in the morning. When her mother found out I was running away, she let me stay the night and said she was going to talk to my mother in the morning. The next day, when my friend and I came in from playing, her mother told me I could stay as long as I liked. However, my friend told me a few days later that her mother felt her father was paying too much attention to me. I didn't want to be the reason for any problems in their home, so I left. As much as I didn't want to go back home, I felt there was no other choice.

Each time I returned home after running away, I was fearful because I knew there was going to be a confrontation. Many times when I returned home, I'd brace myself before knocking on the door because I knew I was going to get a beating, that she'd curse me out and yell at the top of her lungs. When I felt ready, I'd gently knock on the door. It always surprised me how she heard the slightest knock, as if she were standing on the other side of the door waiting for that signal.

I was about twelve or thirteen years old and was fed up with my mother's physical abuse. When I returned after a few days at my girlfriend's house, when my mother opened the door, she blocked me from coming in and said, "What the hell you come back for?"

Then she started cursing and yelling at me and punching me, and then she slapped me in the face. Witnessing as many street fights as I had growing up, getting slapped in the face or spit in the face, to me, was the ultimate form of humiliation. When my mother slapped me in the face that time, it took everything in me not to strike her back.

I was furious as I stood there staring her down, as if to dare her to say another word. I think she was surprised by my reaction and didn't say a word until my father came up to the front area and told her to move and let me in. He shoved her out of the way so he could get by her and grabbed at me to bring me inside. My mother started yelling at him and said, "She ain't bringing her ass back in this house!"

I turned and ran away as quickly as I could and heard my father say, "Come back here." I turned to see him running after me. I knew I could outrun him, although at the same time, I felt sorry for putting him in that situation. But I was determined not to go back into that apartment, so I kept running. I started crying as I ran down the back entrance of the building and jumped down the stairs a flight at a time. Then I heard my dad open the door and continue running after me. By the time I reached the parking lot, he grabbed me by my collar and, out of breath, said, "You ain't going nowhere, you're coming back upstairs with me."

I protested, telling him to let me go, that I didn't want to live there anymore, and that I hated her.

He responded, "Don't you ever let me hear you say that about your mother again."

Reality Sets In

In my naivety, I felt to some extent I understood the remarkable degrees of life, human potential, and a majestic spiritual reality that is beyond human consciousness. However, as I started maturing, I no longer had the luxury of upholding childish daydreams about a life that seemed so far out of my reach.

My curiosity switched from universal knowledge about life to the real world that I had to deal with as a female adolescent living on the streets or in multiple institutions for delinquent or troublesome children. My basic need to survive on my own during my early teenage years became my top concern.

Runaway Child Running Wild

As an adolescent, I didn't understand the lustful antics of men. Some of the men I encountered were strangers. Most were familiar, yet they all felt that my body was theirs for the taking, no matter how hard I tried to resist their masculine gropes. I was totally naive to the effect my developing body had on grown men—even those who were supposed to protect me.

When I was thirteen years old, I ran away from home once again. This time I ventured away from the area I lived in and rode the subway train to The Avenue. Typically, when I went to The Avenue with my friends or sister, we took the bus; this was my first venture riding the subway that far.

I was a bit nervous and couldn't shake the gloomy feeling in the pit of my stomach. It was already getting dark by the time I arrived at The Avenue, and I reluctantly exited the station and descended the stairs into the nearly empty streets.

As I strolled along, to my disappointment, I saw that many of the stores were closed or closing for the night. I continued walking for several more blocks anyway, looking into the store windows.

It seemed the darker the night became, the more derelicts came out of hiding. I realized I was headed into a neighborhood that was unsafe, and I became frightened. The reality set in that I had no place to go, and I started to cry. I certainly wasn't about to look for a safe haven in the neighborhood I'd wandered into. I turned around and started running as fast as I could back to the train station. But I was lost. I'd walked so far I had no idea where I was or how to get back to the subway station.

Panic set in as I looked around trying to get my bearings. Then I saw a "dark shadowy figure" of a tall man standing across the street. I yelled to him for directions to the nearest subway station. He pointed and shouted that there was one about four blocks straight ahead. I quickly took off running in that direction.

As I approached the bottom of the steps to make my way up into the subway station, I heard a Voice from inside me say, "Look over there." I turned and looked across the street to see the "dark shadowy figure" quickly climbing the steps two by two leading up into the subway station. I thought he was climbing the stairs in such a hurry because a train was approaching, so I quickly ran up the steps too.

As I reached for the door handle, the Voice said, "Look inside." I peered through the window and I could clearly see that the station was empty. There was no booth, and the turnstile entrance was fenced in. Plus, there were piles of lumber and other debris on the floor. I quickly turned and hopped down the stairs as quickly as I could. As soon as I reached the bottom step, a police cruiser drove by. I ran wildly to catch up with it while screaming for it to stop. The car stopped, and I ran up to the window. I told the officer that I'd run away from home, I was lost, and I didn't have anywhere to stay.

Did Not Protect, and Served Himself

It was well after 11:00 p.m. when I was sitting in the police station for what seemed like forever, waiting for someone to notify my parents of my whereabouts. I had a genuine surge of remorse and an overwhelming sense of wanting to be home with my family.

Finally, a tall, stocky African American police officer walked up to me and asked my name. He introduced himself, and I pointed out that my father had the same name. I thought the officer must be a pretty cool guy, just like my dad. He told me that he'd spoken to my mother, who had indicated that she did not want me returned to the apartment, that I should be put away somewhere. I asked him if he had spoken with my father. He said, "No, just her."

The officer continued and said that he would have to locate an institution that would take me, but in the meantime, he had to place me in lockup until morning. I was shocked and started crying at the thought of being arrested and jailed. I looked around for the nearest escape route after asking him why I was being arrested. He assured me that I wasn't being arrested, but since I couldn't go back home, I needed to be kept safe until he could place me.

The next morning, the same officer arrived to inform me he'd located a girls' facility that would take me in. He said he would drive me to my apartment because my mother was required to sign off on the paperwork, and I'd be allowed to get some of my clothing. Then he left to go finish some paperwork.

I stayed in lockup until well after mid-morning before we headed out to where I thought was home to do the tasks he'd described earlier. However, on the drive to my mother's apartment, he mentioned that he had a few friends who stayed in the same area, and he wanted to visit with them for a few minutes. He asked if I liked to play handball because his friend would most likely be at the handball court. I didn't respond, as I was thinking, with apprehension, about returning to the apartment. I felt such rage, and I wasn't sure how I'd react when I saw my mother. I was afraid to face her.

Sure enough, when we arrived at the park, the officer spotted his friends on the handball court. We walked over to them, and they greeted each other. He didn't introduce me to any of them, but within a few minutes, one of the men invited me to join the game. I played a few rounds while the officer hung around talking to his friends, and by mid-afternoon, he was ready to leave.

He drove to the projects a few miles away and parked in front of my building. As he was about to get out of the car, I said, "I don't want to go upstairs." I didn't want to see her or hear her voice at all and thought to myself, "Fuck those clothes and her."

He returned to the car about fifteen minutes later and reported he'd seen a lot of similar cases but "that woman takes the cake." I asked if my father was home, and he said no. He then announced he had another stop he wanted to make before driving to the city. By then, it was close to three or four o'clock in the afternoon, and I hadn't eaten all day.

We drove for what seemed like forever. I was hungry and began to wonder where we were headed. Finally, I asked him where we were going and when he was going to take me to the city. He responded that we'd be there soon, but first he wanted to stop by to visit some old friends.

When we finally arrived at some location in Queens, or possibly Brooklyn, the sun was beginning to set. We got out of the car in front of an apartment building and walked down the stairs into what appeared to be a basement that was set up as a juke joint. As I stood by the door, he walked over to the bar and spoke to the bartender. I was uncomfortable being in the dimly lit, smoky basement with adults who were drinking. I was anxious to get going.

The officer called me over to the bar and asked if I wanted something to drink. I said, "No, I don't drink."

He retorted, "Well, you drink sodas, don't you?"

I said, "Not really."

He looked at the bartender and said, "Give her a Coke."

I was thirsty, so I took a big gulp of the beverage. Before taking another sip, I realized the Coke tasted a bit weird. I asked him if he had put alcohol in my drink, and he said, "Oh, it's just a little Bacardi to loosen you up."

That was the last thing I remember before waking up feeling as if someone were hammering a huge wooden stake between my legs.

I was somewhat immobilized and very groggy. I had no idea what was happening to me. I had a hard time opening my eyes and couldn't focus to see where I was. I could not think. There was no instant replay of the incident flashing through my mind—nothing. I was in one of my dream states, and I wasn't even aware I was conscious. I only knew I was still alive because of the excruciating pain throughout my entire body. I screamed out in pain.

Then I heard a male voice telling me to shut up. The next thing I knew, someone placed a pillow over my face and started smothering me. I began twisting and wiggling my upper body to get free in order to breathe and then started clawing and fighting with the person because I thought he was trying to kill me.

All of a sudden I heard someone frantically banging on the door and yelling, "Hey man, what the fuck you doing in there? Open this door, I'm not having that shit in here, you got to go NOW."

I heard the perpetrator reply, "Okay man, it's okay, it's okay."

He took the pillow off my face and told me not to make a sound. I had never been that frightened in my life and all I could do was to scream again. The person on the other end of the door started yelling, "Man open this door, I said open this damn door now!"

The perpetrator said again, "Man, it's okay, we fine, I'll be out in a minute."

The man outside the door said, "Hurry up and get the fuck out of here before I call the cops, motherfucker."

The perpetrator turned and slapped me in the face and then dragged me out of the bed and into the bathroom. He put me in the shower and turned on the cold water. I was dressed only from the top up. I didn't have on my shoes, underwear, or my pants.

When he took me out of the shower, my focus was becoming a little bit clearer. We walked back into the room. I looked around the dingy room and then to the bed, where I spotted blood on the bed sheets. I wondered if it was my blood, but I didn't appear to be bleeding from anywhere. He acted as if he was seeing the blood for the first time also because he snapped, "Shit, you mean to tell me you're a virgin? With a body like that?"

My head was throbbing, and between my legs felt raw, like my insides had been ripped out. I knew the perpetrator had done something nasty to me and I just wanted to drop on the floor and die.

I don't remember how I got dressed. He held me up as we walked out of the room. A man was waiting outside the door and said to the perpetrator, "Man, don't bring your ass back here ever again. I ain't having that shit in here."

When we got to the car, he opened the back door and shoved me in the back seat. Every part of my body was throbbing and in excruciating pain.

A person's knowledge base is at the level of their understanding, meaning, they don't know what they don't know. The word "rape" was not a part of my vocabulary, and I had never had sex before, so it didn't compute in my mind that I'd been raped. But just before I dozed off, I thought, "He slipped me a mickey." I knew without a doubt that whatever happened to me, that officer put something in the drink he gave me.

Welcome to Your New World

We finally arrived at the facility at about one or two o'clock in the morning. The perpetrator woke me up, and when I arose, he turned and pointed a gun in my face and said, "If you tell anyone what happened, I'm coming back to kill you and I'm going to kill your family." He then escorted me inside the institution.

The lady in the reception area took one look at me and said, "What's wrong with this child?"

The officer said, "She's upset because of the fight she had with her mother."

The woman looked as if she didn't believe him, but she didn't challenge him either.

Once the paperwork was completed, he released me into her custody. Once he left the building, she asked me, "What happened?" Then she asked, "Did that man do anything to you, child?"

I couldn't speak. All I could do was cry uncontrollably.

She waited a few moments for me to calm down and told me that I needed to take a shower. She asked if I had any clothes. I shook my head to indicate I did not. She left to retrieve some pajamas, towels, a washcloth, and personal hygiene items. She told me where the showers were and to return to her office to get assigned to a dormitory after I had finished showering.

I spoke no words and followed her directions as ordered. I could hardly walk as I made my way down what seemed like miles of corridor. When I got to the shower room, I began to undress. When I took my pants off, I saw the blood. I was bleeding from between my legs. I started screaming.

The lady rushed into the shower to see me lying on the floor crying. She said, "What's wrong?" I couldn't speak. She looked around and saw my bloody clothing. She said, "Oh child, you starting your period."

She left to get me a sanitary napkin and apparatus. I was so sore I could hardly move. She told me after I showered and put on the pajamas, she'd take me to the infirmary. I sat on the floor in the shower crying until the lady returned, helped me get dressed, went to retrieve a wheelchair and took me to the infirmary.

The staff in the infirmary realized I was in some type of shock. I didn't speak at all, and I couldn't eat, but they made me drink water. All I did was cry the whole time. I stayed in the infirmary for a little over a week before they released me to the dormitory I was assigned to. By then, the shock of that horrible experience was wearing off, and I knew I had to toughen up in order to survive in the facility. The girls in there were from all over the city, and they were hardened, streetwise juvenile delinquents.

The School of Hard Knocks

In my new life at the facility, I became very stoic and developed coping skills to mask my agony. As weary as I was about my life, somewhere deep inside me, I understood that I was embarking on another element of it that was going to be difficult, whether I was ready for it or not. All the hopes and dreams I had for my future vanished. I didn't care what happened to me at that point.

As the days turned into weeks, I was somewhat relieved to be in that facility because my mother could no longer beat on me and I no longer had to look at her or hear her voice. Even so, I felt abandoned. I didn't know what to think about my family. I didn't know what my siblings thought or if they even cared that I was gone. I wondered how my dad felt about the situation and if he was worried about me. Did she even tell him where I was?

I kept waiting for my father to somehow find and rescue me. But I knew if he did, all he would do was take me back to the home I no longer wanted to live in. I saw my father as another victim of my mother's rage and felt sorry for him for having to endure it. He was a good man and didn't deserve to be treated the way she treated him.

After a few weeks, I started phoning home to talk with my dad, but every time I called, my mother answered the phone, so I would hang up.

After suffering years of abuse from my mother and hearing her tell me how she had tried to abort me, I realized when she had me put away, she was rid of me finally. I was forced to survive in a world I didn't comprehend before I was mature enough to appropriately deal with it. I had to survive on my own during an era that was becoming increasingly decadent and threatening for kids, especially girls.

One of the first lessons I learned early on was that I couldn't depend on anyone for my survival but myself. All of my experiences up to that point caused me to become resourceful and heightened my physical senses. I could sniff the air to recognize scents that were different, pleasant, or had a foul odor. A lot of times I had to feel my way through dark spaces. I always listened to sounds in the darkness—footsteps, doors opening and closing, voices—to determine if someone was approaching an area where I was hiding. Noises kept me alert to possible signs of danger. I learned quickly to read people's energy field and observe their mannerisms when they approached me. Living like that caused me to become discerning and to always stay vigilant and aware of my surroundings.

I stayed at the facility for about a year. It was shut down permanently shortly thereafter, so I transferred to another facility in New Jersey, where I stayed until I turned seventeen years old.

Chapter 6

EVERYTHING MAKES SENSE AT SOME POINT

> *The process of finding your true spiritual identity involves looking at your whole life as one long story, trying to find a higher meaning.*
> —James Redfield, *Celestine Insights*

Around the age of twenty-six, I decided to make a radical move out of my home state and away from my family. Some of my friends were moving "down South," where they felt they'd have a better life. I didn't feel close to my siblings and was fed up with the mediocre adult lifestyle I'd fallen into. Many of the people I associated with were heavily into drugs, and I knew I didn't want to be strung out like that.

I yearned for something more positive for my life other than wasting it in the downward spiral of the social ills that plagued the community, and I was fed up with the cold East Coast winters.

After researching a few places I felt offered good employment and creative opportunities (and a warmer climate), I decided to spend the upcoming Labor Day weekend in California. Once there, I fell in love with the city, and a week later, I phoned my mother to inform her I'd be staying permanently.

It took a few months to settle into my new life, but after settling in, I began to observe other mothers and their adult daughters who seemed to have wonderful relationships. I had friends and coworkers who talked lovingly about their relationships with their mothers and about the time they spent together. I envied that. It would have been nice to have that type of relationship with my mom. I desperately wanted to be able to have open, honest conversations with her about our lives and get to know her on a deeper level, as a woman and not just my mom.

My mother was a difficult person to get to know. She always seemed to have her guard up so no one ever got too close to her. In my attempt to break through the ice, I made weekly phone calls home. Instead of greeting her with "Hi, Mom, it's me," I'd start by saying, "Hey, girlfriend." That always seemed to make her smile.

No matter how difficult I believe my childhood was, I was a dutiful daughter, and I never disrespected my parents. Now, don't get me wrong—I felt some type of way about how my mother treated me, and oh yes, I mumbled under my breath many times about it, but never to her face. Even as an adult, when she continued to be who she was, I never felt grown enough to defy her. Although she was a difficult woman to love, I respected her position in my life up to the day she made her transition.

Another Shocking Confession

When my mother died, her sister came from out of town to attend the funeral. That was the first time as an adult that I'd seen her. She had last visited in the sixties when I was around nine or ten years old.

On the day of my mother's funeral, I was in my mother's bedroom looking over the items on the dresser, one of which was a bottle of perfume that I had given her for Mother's Day. Flooded with memories, I began to cry as I opened the bottle and sniffed the Brocade scent. I couldn't believe she still had it and how fresh the scent still smelled after all those years.

As I was reminiscing about the time I gave her the perfume as a child, her sister came into the bedroom and stood by the dresser next to me. I looked up and noticed she was staring into the mirror. In her southern country drawl and with a lip full of snuff, she said, "You know why your mother used to beat you all the time?"

I was taken aback by her question and wanted to be sure I had heard her correctly. I replied, "Excuse me?"

She repeated the question, and before I could respond, she said, "Every time your mother beat you she was beating me. I use to whoop her ass all the time. So when she was beating you she was beating me. You look just like me."

When my aunt shared that revelation, everything made sense. My mother had transferred all the pent up anger she held against her sister onto me. I did remind my mother of someone from her past after all—her own sister, who she must have hated so much for abusing her and who I looked just like.

After the funeral, I flew back home and sought counseling to help deal with the grief. I was not only mourning the loss of my mother's presence here on earth but the opportunities I'd never have to get to know her as a woman.

As much as I wanted to understand her and hear her story in her own voice, I was always so afraid of my mother. I didn't know how to relate or communicate to her in any way other than as a child to a parent. I wanted to have those "girlfriend" moments with her and talk about life. I felt I had a right to know the person she kept hidden.

During a counseling session, I made a comment that I often made in order to rationalize my mother's treatment of me: She was doing the best she could with the knowledge she had. I'd repeated this statement a few times during the session, and the counselor finally remarked, "Oh, no, she doesn't get off that easily, she is still responsible for her actions."

Her statement took me aback because it brought alive the fact that I'll never have the opportunity to have those difficult conversations with my mother or to ask her the questions I need answers to. I will never have the chance to get her perspective about what her aspirations for her life were before she met my father.

It took me three years of counseling to work through my grief and issues with my mother to get to the point of forgiving her as well as to cope with the death of my father eleven months after my mother made her transition. In spite of what the counselor believed about holding my mother responsible for her actions, I knew deep in my heart that she was the product of her environment and she treated me the way she was treated. That awareness enabled me to genuinely begin to understand her as a woman and enabled me to accept her for who she was.

For those who are reading this book and have parents who are still alive, I hope that you will make a way to have a heart-to-heart talk with them about your issues of concern. Part of the healing process for some of you will be to respectfully have those difficult conversations.

Even if your parents don't want to talk about it, you can write a letter, take them out to dinner, send a card—do what you have to—to begin the healing process. It's important for you to gently reach out and make your parent(s) aware of your need to discuss some issues that are important to you and your healing.

Most importantly, when you're able to, let them know that you genuinely forgive them. I realize that can be a big leap, and I don't suggest doing it until you're in a place where you can be authentic about it. That may require doing some forgiveness work during your private times of meditation and reflection. The Spirit will guide you accordingly. Don't rush the process. Remember, you're chipping away at a proverbial iceberg.

Most of the time, abusive parents are the product of abuse themselves, and they too have unresolved issues stemming from their childhood. Facing the truth of one's abuse takes a special kind of courage. In order for you to be an emotionally healthy adult, the truth must be dealt with so the healing can begin. An abused child who does not face the truth of their traumatic childhood as an adult is in great danger of repeating the cycle of abuse—just as my mother did when she projected the abuse from her sister onto me.

At the time of counseling, I felt I was ready to face the truth about my adverse childhood experiences and I was on my journey to heal the emotional wounds I still carried. But I didn't realize how deeply I was wounded, and counseling only touched the tip of that proverbial iceberg.

The Bigger Picture

When I was in my forties, I took a class at a local church that was quite insightful. The instructor conducted an activity in which the class was required to anonymously write a few words on a piece of paper about the worst thing our parents did or said to us. The purpose of the exercise was to begin healing from painful emotional baggage, which many of us still carried around.

After a brief meditation led by the instructor and dwelling on the assignment, I thought back to my childhood, the time when my mother stomped me. But as I was about to jot down those thoughts, another thought occurred to me. The worst thing my mother said to me as a child was the story she told about how she tried to abort me.

Slowly I wrote, as if dazed, "my mother told me how she tried to abort me."

I quickly folded the paper and placed it in the bowl that was being passed around the room. I was surprised that the thought was still just as painful, more than thirty years later. The memory reopened the emotional wound. I felt like crying and wanted to leave the room, but instead I sat stiffly in the chair trying very hard not to give in to the emotion.

After the instructor read each note, she'd pause for a moment of silent prayer before reading the next note. When she read the statement written by me, the whole class gasped, and I shivered a little in unison. I felt as if

I was going to pass out. That was the first time since my childhood that I had heard those words spoken.

After the instructor read the last note, we set the papers on fire in the bowl. This was a symbolic gesture of destroying the negative energy associated with those collective painful memories. If only life were that easy.

Although it was somewhat upsetting recalling that memory, I did not want to fall into that rabbit hole by dwelling on the experience again. Yes, I felt some kind of way about how I was treated as a child, but I wasn't about to dissect my mother's life or judge whether or not she lived according to any particular standards. There are both good and bad ingredients from both my parents that I must have needed in order to develop my human character.

Through all the traumatic experiences, I'd learned to trust the spiritual process unequivocally. I viewed the Spirit's guidance as pieces to the puzzle of my life that worked together for my good. Wherever these pieces, or breadcrumbs, led—whether to a bookstore to purchase a book to read, a television or radio program to listen to, or a workshop or conference to attend—the answer or message I needed in that moment was there. I just had to show up.

Chapter 7

VITALIZED, NO LONGER A VICTIM

The broken adult child can be healed once they recognize the untapped potential that lies dormant in them.

Victimhood can be an excuse to not take responsibility for your healing. It seems safer to lick the wounds, wallow in self-pity, and blame others for how you turned out. My mother's harsh comments throughout my life made me feel worthless, as if nothing I had to say was important. I felt that she didn't care about what I did with my adult life.

As much as I wanted her approval, she always seemed to find something hurtful to say. When my child was born prematurely, she proclaimed, "It doesn't weigh more than a pound of ground beef." After I moved to California, when I'd call home to ask her advice about something, her remarks would entail "you made your bed, you got to lie in it," or one of her other favorite sayings, "your foot don't fit no limb." What the heck does that mean, anyway? All these years later, I still haven't figured that one out.

It's important for parents to realize the depth of impact their criticisms can have on the psyche of their children. I didn't pay attention to the multidimensional effects the emotional abuse had on me until well into my early adult life. After a few years of implementing personal development strategies that helped me come out of my shell, I finally felt comfortable sharing my authentic voice. I began attending professional development courses that were sponsored either at work or off-site. I read plenty of self-help books, listened to audio by various motivational speakers, and attended workshops to help boost my self-esteem.

I made a bold decision when I stepped outside of my comfort zone and responded to an ad in a local newspaper for a cohosting position on a weekend talk radio show that aired on a popular Christian radio station. It was an opportunity for me to test my ability to express myself freely while engaging in meaningful conversations. I was invited to the studio to meet the host and the cohost. I was offered the role and relished the time I spent preparing for and cohosting the show. It was exhilarating, my self-confidence was elevated, and I realized that people really did want to hear what I had to say!

A Journey of Personal Healing and Spiritual Evolution

I began hosting my own talk radio show at the same radio station and eventually moved to Internet radio. While doing Internet radio, I would often get requests from people to be on the show to talk about their new book, and I sought out motivational guests for the show as well. Many talked about what or who inspired them, and many of the conversations were about ancient wisdom and metaphysical and spiritual philosophy. I wasn't familiar with those theories but became curious, as many of the guests seemed genuinely happy and peaceful.

After I recorded a show with John Randolph Price, the founder of World Healing Day and the Quartus Foundation, my curiosity got the best of me, and I took a sabbatical so I could learn more about the New Thought philosophies. I started meeting people who were on that spiritual journey, and one man and his wife became my spiritual mentors. They helped me tremendously to understand spiritual principles and how everything I've been through has led up to the spiritual awakening I was beginning to experience.

My thirties were spent diligently working to establish my own identity. It was not easy to finally break free from the mental shackles that kept my mind bound to my mother's opinion of me. I went on a seven-year journey of enlightenment, during which I purged old attitudes and behaviors that challenged my beliefs about the Christian religion. Listening to gospel music was a lifeline for me while I was going through my trials and tribulations. There was always a song for every mood or emotion I had, and the music helped me stay in a state of worship. On the other hand, when I discovered New Thought music, I actually felt one with God. I felt empowered and connected to the Source of Life. The words were like seeds being planted in soil.

On this quest, my zest for life began to return. I felt reborn, and I was hopeful. As I began to study New Thought books on the metaphysical, ancient wisdom, and spiritual philosophies, it was confirmed that this spiritual awakening was the greater calling for my life. I rejoiced at the thought that God had assigned a heavenly host of angels to protect me in my ignorance as I meandered through life trying to "find myself."

I desperately needed a new way to rewire my brain because my typical go-to resources were no longer adequate. I didn't want counseling because I was fed up with talking about the past and reliving those memories, which seemed counterproductive. I didn't want to read more self-help books, and I didn't want to hear more redundant church sermons. There had to be a better way to purge my mind of the garbage I'd been dragging around, but I was ignorant as to how to do it.

Maya Angelou wrote, "My willingness to do so was hampered by an abounding ignorance of how it should be done." Boy, did I feel ignorant and like I was at a crossroad. I wondered, do I stay on the same path and keep doing what I've always done, or do I explore an unknown new path?

I no longer wanted to be held hostage to the past or spend the rest of my life dealing with my unresolved childhood issues. I had endured enough mental anguish and suffering in silence, and I was ready to be free from the same old drama and issues I had been dealing with for far too many years. It was time to let go of the playing-the-victim role and the self-absorbed, self-sabotaging pity parties.

There were times I would get so depressed thinking about all the "what ifs" and "how different my life would be if only" scenarios. That type of stinking thinking served no productive purpose and only kept me immobilized, stuck in a rut looking at life through the rearview mirror. I had another one of those "come let us reason together" moments, and I prayed for answers like I had never prayed before.

I still did not know who I was as a woman and the type of person I was becoming. I still viewed myself based on other people's opinions of me—their definition of my life as a mother, wife, employee, businesswoman, and sister. I functioned every day as I was socially conditioned to and masked my utter dissatisfaction.

In my quest for healing, I did a lot of soul-searching and took an inventory of my life. I wanted to know how people who knew me for some time viewed me. I talked to people, but only those I trusted to give an honest, unbiased assessment of my character. Their input helped me see areas I needed to improve.

I was on this new journey of spiritual awakening and felt like a blank slate wiped clean, yet there was a speck of the old writing still visible on the slate. I searched for New Thought churches in the area and found a Unity Church that I attended for a while. Then I began visiting Spiritual Living churches and that doctrine resonated with me. I had my astrological birth chart made. That helped me to not only understand my character but also to potentially find direction for my life in terms of possible career choices.

Keep in mind that sometimes you have to deviate from the norm in order to reach your sanity. The choice really is up to you.

Chapter 8

THE ABCs YOU DIDN'T LEARN IN SCHOOL

Every wounded adult who harbors unresolved issues from their childhood may or may not realize that those issues are controlling the ABCs—attitude, belief, and conduct—of their life.

Simply Defined

Attitude

According to Merriam-Webster's online dictionary, the word "attitude" means a settled way of thinking or feeling about someone or something, typically one that is reflected in a person's behavior.

I'm sure many of you may have heard the expression, "Your attitude determines your altitude." If you're holding on to animosity, regret, or bitterness from unresolved childhood issues or disempowering memories about your past traumatic experiences, that attitude will show up in some way or another in your life, whether in how you treat others or how you feel about yourself.

When you hold on to strong negative feelings, you are poisoning yourself and building toxins in your body that will manifest in the form of some type of disease, which will impact your overall physical or emotional well-being. The same energy it takes to hold on to feelings of anger, hate, or sorrow can be used to heal your wounds by using it to adopt an attitude of love, peace, acceptance, and forgiveness.

Your feelings are your thermometer to your attitude, and…your life is the mirror to your attitude.

—Piercarla Garusi

Belief

Merriam-Webster's online dictionary defines "belief" as a state or habit of mind in which trust or confidence is placed in some person or thing; something that is accepted, considered to be true, or held as an opinion.

Your belief about yourself, even if it's someone else's opinion, is what you accept as true for you. I once heard someone say, "It's not what you call me but what I answer to." If you are called stupid, worthless, or any other negative adjective, and you accept that as your reality, then you answer that call by becoming a stupid worthless person living a stupid worthless life. You've essentially given away your power to the people who call you that. The vibrations you release into the Universe will boomerang right back to you. You will make sure you self sabotage anything that goes against that negative programming by putting yourself in situations that set you up to fail, so you can validate being stupid and worthless.

Take your power back and begin to fix your faulty programming. It's time for you to update the software in your mind. Begin to form a daily habit that motivates you and spiritually uplifts you, and notice how your mind begins to free itself from the disempowering thought patterns. Try it for thirty days and note how your attitude and belief begin to change and how much better you begin to feel about yourself.

What you believe about your life will become the world you create. You will draw into your world everything that lines up with your thoughts, whether good or bad. Choose your words wisely and then write a new script for your life. Focus on what is good about you and believe that. Affirm your new life.

Your beliefs become your thoughts, your thoughts become your words, your words become your actions, your actions become your habits, your habits become your values, your values become your destiny.

—Mahatma Ghandi

Conduct

According to Merriam-Webster's online dictionary, "conduct" is defined as causing (oneself) to act or behave in a particular and especially in a controlled manner.

When I think about conduct, I also think about self-control. As a result of adverse childhood experiences, so many people behave in ways that are self-destructive, and they actually believe that because they're hurting they have to hurt others, be it verbally, physically, or emotionally.

Until you realize the problem is with you, and until you deal with your issue head on, it is still going to haunt you. Conduct your everyday self in a manner worthy of your authentic nature. Behave as if all things are working together for our good, and watch the magic unfold.

Conduct yourself in ways that demonstrate you are a survivor, not someone who is defeated by their past trauma. Going forward, when you speak about your life, your words should always be life affirming.

Conduct is the best proof of character.

—Niccolo Machiavelli

How I Learned My ABCs

My mother's attitudes, beliefs, and conduct demonstrated to me anger, fear, unrequited love, anti-social behavior, and loneliness. My father's attitudes, beliefs, and conduct demonstrated to me authenticity, unconditional love, strength, compassion, hard work, love of music, spirituality, and family unison.

My attitudes, beliefs, and conduct were built on fragments from the environment I grew up in. It wasn't until I became aware of my spiritual identity that I understood some of my attitudes, beliefs, and conduct about life were faulty and would not stand the test of time.

When I understood and assimilated into my consciousness that I am one with a supreme power higher than myself, that awareness eventually contributed to my shift in perception from blaming my parents for my adverse childhood experiences to understanding their history. That awareness led me to seek a solution to my childhood heartache, and eventually created in me a clean heart of genuine forgiveness and unconditional love for them.

The time and effort you devote to building yourself up through your daily implementation of personal development strategies will aid you in evolving beyond the stereotypical dynamics of a dysfunctional childhood, and you will break away from tribal thinking and patterns of behavior.

The child in you may still want your parents to give you what you didn't get in your childhood, but it's time for the adult you to acknowledge that your parents may have been or may still be emotionally immature and can't be people they are not. We think they should have done better, however, they may not have always known how to do better. Some parents made an honest attempt at raising children and made mistakes out of ignorance; and yes, some parents may deliberately have abused their kids as a result of their own adverse childhood experiences.

I guarantee you and I have made parenting mistakes and will continue to make mistakes as we adjust our parenting styles to meet the basic needs of children born in such a socially dynamic and technologically savvy global economy.

Whatever it is that you needed as a child and did not get, whether that be security, guidance, love, attention, or whatever it is for you, at this point in your life, you can't go back and get what you didn't get in your childhood. Wasting years of energy wishing things had been different is counterproductive. You can't rewrite the past—the past is over and done with. Who you are today is all that matters. Who are you? Will you forever let your past circumstances define who you are, how you think, and how you behave? I'm here to clearly state that you are not your past. Whatever you wanted from your parents that you didn't get, give that to your children and break the cycle of generational dysfunction in your family's lineage.

It's hard to see beyond your conditions when you're in the midst of it, especially if you're looking through rose-tinted glasses. This is all the more reason it's important to turn to professionals to provide a perspective that gets you thinking outside of the box so you can find a solution that will help you navigate your way out of the mindboggling maze of dismay. Make peace with your past and kiss it goodbye. Step into the glorious new life that is waiting for you to show up!

Stop the foolish thinking that conditions hold you, it is you holding onto conditions. Quite your self-pity, blaming others, and saying you are the victim of circumstances.

—Delmer Eugene Croft

BELIEVER

Be who you are divinely ordained to be; that should always be the main goal for your life.

Elevate your consciousness to the awareness of your authentic nature and live from that place. You are an ethereal being wrapped in a physical body. If you are ready to let go of traumatic experiences that happened in your childhood, it's time to change the way you view yourself.

Learn to affirm and empower yourself. What are you calling yourself when you talk to yourself? Don't allow other peoples' definitions of you to become your reality. Begin to integrate spiritual knowledge and practices into your everyday activities, and do more than just recite traditional religious dogma. Build yourself up on what you're learning to be true about you. You are not a carbon copy, you are a Divine original, so be your authentic self.

Instead of going with the flow and doing the same old things and getting the same old results of the same old misery and the same old story, get a new life. Make a concerted effort to associate with people who are evolving along your new journey: likeminded people who are searching for the true meaning of life. It's time to dance to the tune of a different drummer. Find your tune. Once you do, I hope you dance through life as if you own the world—and you do. You own the world you live in, so be the queen in your Queendom.

Every relationship you have is for a reason and a season, even that with your parents. Sometimes we don't always have to know the reason why. It's more important to learn the lesson so you can move on to the next degree of glory for your life. Treasure the relationships that empower and support your personal and spiritual development. If a person tries to enter your Queendom and they don't meet those basic criteria, their season is up the second they show you who they are. Beware of wolves in sheep's clothing—they are roaming about seeking whoever is gullible.

Very little will change in your life if you don't recognize how the Spirit shows up to guide you in piecing together the puzzle for your life. You are an Ethereal Being having a human experience. What happened back then does not preclude you from being the best you that you can be today. You just have to make the effort. You may not see the big picture or have all the answers, but if you follow the breadcrumbs that show up in your life and if you continue to press on toward the mark of the Higher Calling, you will be transformed, and your mind will be renewed.

Everything you need to overcome any obstacle is already inside you. Nothing is impossible. So pick yourself up—your Queendom is awaiting your arrival!

Repeat the affirmation below, as it can be a useful tool for you as you begin your journey of evolution. Write it down somewhere and read it aloud every day until you have memorized it in your heart and it becomes your new reality.

The Spirit within me makes all things new.
Every negative thought or condition is erased from
my experience.
I am aware of my union with Good. I am conscious
of my
oneness with Life.
I expect more prosperity, more happiness, more
harmony than ever before.
I walk in the joy of ever-increasing good.[5]

Chapter 9
REVELATIONS

> *No matter where you go in life, until you deal with your baggage, all that garbage travels with you.*

My Sister Shares Her Thoughts

At the age of sixty-three, my sister wanted to share her impressions about growing up in our household. I didn't know what to expect from her, as we never had had an in-depth conversation about our mother. I always felt my sister esteemed my mother to some extent, simply because she rarely spoke negatively about her to me. I didn't feel compelled to share my deep feelings with my very spiritual sister. Maybe it was because the little girl in me felt her big sister would warn her again about the Bible verse on honoring your mother and about the bus running me over if I spoke ill of her.

As we began talking about her memories, my sister spoke freely. She thanked God for the years and the tears because it "toughened her up." She shared that she felt her values were distorted, and she was scarred in her heart and mindset in regard to the type of woman she wanted to become.

In high school, she wanted to be a nurse, but she didn't finish the LVN program because of the challenges she had while living at home. She was trying to find a balance between her social and professional ambitions and didn't have proper guidance to steer her in the right direction. She began to take an interest in men, specifically one who enticed her to leave home to get married before she was equipped to cope in an adult world.

Mother had not been very open with her, and my sister felt Mother "could have been more compassionate and loving; and not so tough as if she were raising all boys." Because mother was so harsh on her, it had an impact on the choices and decisions she made. She wanted to be loved for who she was and couldn't find that compassion and understanding from the people she went to school with or hung out with. She looked for love and friendship in other people who didn't appreciate her, and in some cases, took advantage of her. Subsequently, my sister was down on herself, which impacted relationships with the men in her life. She chose men who, instead of lifting her up, put her down and abused her.

She shared what I thought was an interesting perspective: she felt Mother was selfish. Although I had never looked at it that way, I had to agree with her. She thought what our mother saw in us was what she didn't like about herself when she was growing up in the South, meaning Mother saw elements of herself in us. My sister felt that whatever good we were capable of doing, Mother didn't nurture that talent in us.

My sister desperately wanted Mother to acknowledge her and to tell her that she loved her as a person and a woman, not just as one of her daughters. For her, to hear Mother tell her that she loved her, the woman she was and was becoming, would have validated her transition into womanhood.

She recalled the time when she asked Mother if she loved her.

Mother had responded, "I love all of you."

My sister didn't want to hear that; she wanted to know if Mother loved her, individually, in spite of her faults. She wanted to know if she lived up to Mother's expectations of what she wanted her to do with her life or even what Mother thought of her as a woman. Mother never gave her a clear answer like, "Yes, daughter, I love you." It was always, "I love all my children." My sister needed to have that motherly support, to know that her mother felt that "no matter what you do, I still love you."

My sister shared with me that she found acceptance in other family members, namely my father's niece whose house she was always at and where she found solace. She felt my cousin's house was always open, and that my cousin was understanding and very accepting of people—no one person was better than the next.

My sister said something I thought was very profound and that was, "When you love somebody, you love them, you don't tell somebody you're not welcome here in my house, you can't come here, or your friends can't call you on the telephone. It's a lot of those little things that harden your spirit and turn you away from humanity and learning about what trust and what true love is all about."

I asked her to answer the following questions:

What unresolved issues are still lingering from your childhood, and how have those issues impacted you as an adult?

Honestly, I don't know. I thank God that the peace I experience has taken away a lot of my hurt feelings about that. But I never had a daughter to have that type of relationship with. I can't see myself like that with her or to express myself that way to share that kind of love with her.

But I think I would say, while growing up, hearing that I was never going to be more than this or that scarred me; along with the whippings with the ironing cord, being told to get out, and not being financially supported didn't nurture me or help me to mature.

What do you wish Mom had said to you?

That she loved me and for her to hold me. I wanted to be able to lay my head on her chest and know that she loved me. To know that it wasn't her duty or something she felt she had to do but that it was genuine. It would have been nice to have her say, yes, I do love you, or even for us to go out to dinner or her fix my favorite meal; that would have been very nice to have.

No one really knows my hurt and pain. I don't share that with anybody but the Lord. I think the most profound thing I'd say about it today, even in the spirit, if she could just hold me and let me lay my head on her chest, that would cover a multitude of sin, a multitude of hurt and pain, a multitude of neglect for not being responsible. A hug goes a long way, even when you're weak. Or saying I love you and I do care about you. Even if she said I love you all, but I do love you. If she would have just done that, I think that would have been enough to carry me the rest of my life. No matter what I went through, I would have been able to know my mother loved me.

If you could say anything to her now, what would you say?

That I love you and I want to come back home. I didn't want to live out there on my own after I got married and divorced at such a young age. I wanted to go back home. I wanted to feel like I was welcomed back home, not just by Daddy but by Mommy too, and I didn't get that. No matter what we went through, we should always be able to come back home.

Because I felt I couldn't go back home, I did what I had to do in order to survive and it deterred me from doing a lot of things that I could have done maybe a little better. I had to learn how to live to raise my son, to keep one step from living on the streets. Even though I was strong in my faith, I was weak as a woman. In my heart and mind, I was piecing together her life and her footsteps, comparing some of the ways I was going in my life and how I was doing as a woman. I didn't want to be like Mommy.

Finish this sentence: Mom, I forgive you for_____.

I forgive you for not understanding your daughter. I forgive you. I just plain forgive you because I will always love you, and you're my mother. I forgive you for not understanding me as I was coming into my womanhood, whether I was becoming a homely woman, a righteous woman, a good woman, or a bad woman.

One of the points made during my schooling to become a certified drug, alcohol, and substance abuse specialist was that everyone wants to be validated, especially by their parents. Who doesn't want validation from their parent? Who doesn't want to hear their parent say I love you and I'm proud of you for the person you're becoming?

It definitely takes a village to raise children. Family members, school, after school activities, team sports, and other outside professional organizations and resources can all be part of the support system for a child. The more support a child has, the more resilient he or she becomes to the harmful effects of adverse childhood experiences.

As difficult as it may be raising children, it's easy to categorize parents as good or bad when parenting is a complex endeavor, a myriad of actions, reactions, attitudes, beliefs, and conduct. When a woman becomes a mother and a man a father, it's important for them to understand the task they've undertaken. That cute little baby will hopefully become an adult child who will be the byproduct of that complex network whether it's a good or bad environment.

After talking with my sister and hearing her perspective, my feelings about my mother didn't change, but I did wonder momentarily if my mom ever realized how much my sister needed her nurturing, and later in life, her guidance and support. I thought it was too bad that she missed the opportunity to consciously shape the woman my sister was to become.

My heart went out to my sister because she had suffered in silence. She suffered so much emotionally, and

I regretted that we hadn't spoken about the issue sooner so she could have released some of her repressed feelings. Her pain was very real and it was evident in her voice as she shared with me how deeply she was scarred. Listening to her share her heart touched me deeply, and when I hung up the phone after speaking with her, I couldn't stop the tears from flowing. I was saddened because she loved my mother dearly and desperately wanted that love reciprocated. I wished in that moment I was nearer to her so I could give her a hug.

I recently spoke to my brother about his perspective of our childhood. He knew he was the favorite child, and he said he didn't have any issues with my mom. His issues were with my dad because my dad did not want him to go into professional boxing. My dad was a lightweight boxer in his younger years and knew all too well how brutal boxing could be. He wanted to protect his son from the damaging effects of the sport.

My brother did reconcile his differences with my dad. He felt we had a good foundation growing up in a two-parent household and that helped him to change his life around when he made bad choices during his teenage years.

However, my brother believes because my parents weren't educated beyond high school, and the quality of education was most likely inferior, they didn't know how to intellectually or patiently explain the consequences of our actions. Instead, they just said "don't do this or don't do that."

When I asked his opinion about the beatings, he shared it was their way of disciplining their kids to get control of them. He shared that he thought my mother was justified when she beat us because there had to be a motive for her to do so. He didn't feel she was taking her frustrations out on her children or my dad. He felt the extreme beatings were a result of us running away and therefore infuriating our mother because she had to chase and catch us in order to beat us.

As a parent myself, one of my goals is for my children to know and feel that they are unequivocally loved. I tell them "I love you" every day I speak with any one of them. I have open and honest conversations with them, share my life experiences, and support them through their life experiences. Whatever I wanted or needed emotionally and didn't get through my mother, I give that and more to my children.

One of my children is a lot like me in that he has an inquiring mind and constantly asks questions about my life growing up or my life with his father. Sometimes the memories are painful for me to talk about, but I realize that if he's inquiring, he has a right to know. However, because he's so much like me, at times he'll probe to the finite degree, but if the questioning gets too intense, I just let him know that we can talk later—I'm done for now!

When your babies come into adulthood, they are bound to have questions about their life growing up with you. When they do approach you, you should be ready to give them an honest answer. If you need time to address a painful inquiry, then say so, but don't avoid addressing the question in a timely manner. Inquiring minds should inquire, and your child deserves an answer even if it hurts to relive those memories. It could very well be a therapeutic step to healing old wounds.

Chapter 10
CONVERSATIONS WITH THE LITTLE GIRL WITHIN

At the conclusion of the Reiki session I mention in the Prelude, the practitioner suggested that I have a conversation with the little girl within me to see what other messages she had. Although I was apprehensive at first, the more I thought about it, the idea began to make sense. It became clear that I needed to do it, especially after I interviewed my sister. I really did need to hear what other message Little Shirley had for me.

I was hesitant, as I had not deliberately attempted to connect to any entity before. I viewed posing questions to the Universe as connecting to the Source of Life and used that analogy to make it more feasible to have that conversation with Little Shirley.

I prepared myself to have the conversation by prayerfully asking the Spirit to reveal what Little Shirley wanted to say and to not let me get in the way but to be an open vessel to receive whatever needed to be revealed. I let it go.

Several days later, as I was preparing for my journaling session, I took a few moments to set the intention to be open to hearing the Voice and quiet my mind of the chatter. I liken this practice to tuning in to a radio frequency and clearing the static so I can tune in to a clear channel to receive the message that wants to come up. On the morning of the conversation with Little Shirley, I wasn't focused specifically on dialoguing with her, however, no sooner than I relaxed into my meditation mode, I heard her speak abruptly. She came through very clearly, and it surprised me for a moment.

In all honesty, I should not have been surprised at the intensity of anger that came up from her, but I was. I don't know that I would have ever had the courage to say to my parents the things Little Shirley revealed.

I knew that, as a child, I had stuffed a lot of my anger deep inside because I didn't feel there was a safe human outlet to express my anger nor to seek advice among family and close friends, especially after my sister told me that I "could get run over by a bus" if I spoke badly about my mother.

Subsequently, as I moved forward in life, I buried my true feelings. I understand now that even though I thought I had forgiven my mother, this adult child had indeed still been harboring bitterness from her adverse childhood experiences. These are the questions and authentic answers from the conversation with Little Shirley:

What would Little Shirley say to her mother and father?

Mommy, you were so cruel and hateful, I don't know why you had to be that way. You hated me for no reason of my own, and you put so much fear in me when all I wanted to do was love you and learn from you. I wanted to have fun with you, to talk with you, to laugh with you, and feel comforted. I trusted you, and you beat all the love I had for you right out of me.

I didn't like coming home from school because of the gloom and doom in the atmosphere. When I walked in the door, I could sense whether you were home or not, and I was glad when I came home and you were gone.

You beat on my father and made his life a living hell. He was a good man who also trusted you with his love. I loved my daddy, and every time I saw you hit him, I hated you more and more. I prayed for the day he would hit you back, but he never did. I wanted him to beat you like you beat me.

What would the adult Shirley say to her mother and father?

Mom, it took a long time and a lot of introspective work to learn how to forgive and love you. But it was worth the effort. As a grown woman, I understand how a person can become paralyzed by the pains and ghosts from their past. I can only imagine the horrible things you witnessed and endured growing up in the era you did.

I knew you were hurting inside and I felt sorry for you. I wish you could have shared some of it with me so I could have understood you, the woman. Maybe talking about it would have taken some of the pressure off you. I loved you so much, Mommy, and all I wanted to do was to show you how much I appreciated you. I wanted to shine so you could be proud of me. I wanted to see your face glow with pride because I was your child.

Mommy, your Spirit woke me up at two o'clock in the morning a few days before you made your transition and let me know you wanted to see me. You had all of your favorite children around you, but you waited for me to travel from over three thousand miles away to be with you. I saw that tear fall from your eye when you heard my voice. Even though when I was at the hospital you never spoke a word, I knew then in those last few moments that I was special to you, indeed. I hope you liked the blue carnations.

Daddy, in your own way you taught me some of the most fundamental principles about life. Such things like respecting myself, and respecting my elders, loving "The Master," and maintaining the connection to family. I know you had a hard life too, Daddy, and I appreciate the fact that you stayed through the storms and didn't abandon your family. You will always be my hero.

What is the adult Shirley conveying to Little Shirley in this moment?

Little girl, your curiosity about life will be satisfied through an amazing set of experiences, and all your questions will be answered. There is nothing wrong with you—you're special, and your light will always shine. You were so far ahead of your time, people didn't understand you, but that's okay. You're perfect, and one day they will understand.

You danced to the beat of a different drummer, and as long as we're on this planet, we'll keep on dancing to the music we hear. Thank you, for your courage and determination; thank you, for enduring all that you have; and thank you, for seeking the greater good in life. I adore you, Shirley.

The conversation ended as abruptly as it began. I sat, lingering in a meditated state that felt as if I were engulfed in some type of bliss. I had no immediate emotional response to the conversation.

After the meditative state wore off, I started crying. The tears just flowed. I also noticed a strong stirring sensation in the third chakra region, right in the pit of my stomach. And I felt proud to some extent that Little

Shirley stood up to my mother by expressing those things. Although it was liberating, I was truly shocked at the intensity of anger she had. That bothered me to some extent because as an adult, I consciously didn't feel that strongly, or at least I thought I didn't. But by hearing her authentically express what I'd never dare say was somewhat of a relief, and I was at peace with that.

The experience gave me an enormous sense of gratitude and respect for my parents. I thought about how they must have faced horrendous obstacles in their lives yet maintained their determination to survive and do their best to ensure we'd have a better life than what they had, even if they didn't know how to demonstrate it. That thought reignited my aspirations to keep my promise to make something good of my life so their efforts would be in vain. I thought the nature of the conversation resulted in forgiveness and healing for the wounded child, along with:

1. Little Shirley finally verbalizing her anger issues.

2. I, Adult Shirley, understanding and honoring my parent's history, and the woman my mother was. I felt I was able to have that small conversation with my mother that I didn't have before she transitioned. The conversation was a chance for me to convey what I needed her to know and what I understood about her, as a woman and not just my mother.

3. Saluting Little Shirley for her courage to stay true to her authentic nature at such a young age and thanking her for letting me know that "she's happy now and we got this."

4. Becoming stirred by the experience and deeply moved. I felt an enormous sense of peace.

All Said and Done

At some point, you have to grow up, deal with the hand you've been dealt, and determine to turn that adverse childhood experience into stepping-stones to a brighter future. It doesn't matter so much how we start out in life—when it's all said and done, what's more important is what we do in between the start and finish of our life. You can choose to waste your time in self-pity and look for excuses and vices to stay stuck in a rut, or you can choose a divinely tailor-made solution that harmonizes you and moves you into your destiny.

Very few people realize that a shift in their mindset has to occur in order for change to happen in their life. Change is generally uncomfortable but necessary if you want to move beyond past circumstances.

Many adults are stuck at some traumatic point in their childhood and continue to suffer emotionally from their childhood issue. Many times, their dysfunctions are passed down to their children in some way, shape, or form. Subsequently, the dysfunction continues from one generation to the next.

Throughout my adult life, old records kept playing over and over in my head, and I'd constantly hear my mother's voice berating and belittling me every time I was on the cusp of a significant accomplishment, and then I would do something to self sabotage.

What I didn't realize at the time was that I had forgiven my mother's behaviors, but I had not forgiven myself for the resentment I still had toward her for my adverse childhood experiences. It's easy to say you forgive and forget, but in reality, the process of forgiveness is much deeper than a simple cliché. It is serious business and takes work if you really want to let go of whatever the object of forgiveness is.

Once my parents made their transition, it didn't seem to make sense for me to continue feeling some kind of way about my adverse childhood experiences. My parents' lives were over, and what was done was done. As far as I was concerned, no new revelation was going to change that fact.

I realized that no matter how much society had changed and technology had advanced, or how much more accessible information was, compared to ten, twenty, or thirty years ago, my parents had parented their children the way they knew how during their era. They were struggling with their own issues of life and could not give us what they didn't have.

Some professional counselors believe that parents should be held responsible for their actions that impede the emotional stability of their child, and I agree with that wholeheartedly. Even though our parents may have been wounded as a result of their upbringing, I believe somewhere in their consciousness, they do know the difference between what they were doing that is right and what they were doing that is wrong, even if only for a split second.

They made a conscious decision to hurt us because they were hurt and never healed from that. In addition, in some instances, family members cover up, excuse, and keep family secrets that only perpetuate the cycle of dysfunction.

Yes, our parents' actions and those of others who violated us have left us wounded and scarred. Wounds heal, and the scars can be removed if you are willing to do the work necessary to heal. If you don't, you're jeopardizing your future by staying blindsided by your past.

The era my mother and father grew up in and raised their children in was so much different than the era I grew up in and raised my children in. Subsequently, the era my children are raising their children in is different than the era they grew up in. This is the ebb and flow of life. Each generation should grow and learn from and build on the previous generations' problems, finding solutions that make life better for everyone in their sphere of influence.

My parents didn't have the insight, information, or intentions that I have as an adult. Their mission was to survive. My quest was for knowledge so that I could make a better life for myself and pass the information to my children so they would have a better life than I did.

As much as I loved being a mother, heck, I made a lot of mistakes while parenting my children, and I'm sure they have some stories they can tell about me. More than anything, though, I hope they know that my goal as their mother is to be a role model of integrity and endurance, and to always be available to them, supportive of them, and loving to them.

My advice to anyone who desires to begin the process of making peace with their past is, if your parents are still alive, yes, respectfully hold them accountable for their actions. I waited too late to have the necessary conversations with my mom, and I didn't get to share what was in my heart with her. One reason I wanted to wait was because I didn't think I was emotionally ready to face her, and I was still afraid to speak my truth to my mother. Secondly, I thought I had time to do it later.

I was kept in the dark about my mother's illness and I didn't expect her to die as suddenly as she did. Shortly after the Northridge earthquake in January of 1994, I received a phone call that she was in the hospital and in and out of consciousness. The caller said my mother asked, "Did Shirley get here yet?"

I replied, "Tell her I'm on my way."

It was the middle of winter, and all the flights heading into New York had been cancelled. I took an Amtrak train from California into New York City, and I arrived at the hospital three days later.

When I walked into the room, I said, "Hey girlfriend, what's going on?"

My mother didn't respond. She was more out of consciousness than in, but a few tears flowed from her eyes.

I was in shock but kept talking to her anyway. One of the last questions I asked her was if she wanted me to bring her some flowers. She shook her head yes. I asked what type and began naming all sorts of flowers that she didn't agree to. Finally, I asked, "Well do you want some blue carnations then?"

She shook her head yes.

She transitioned the next day. At the end of her funeral service, the mortician walked over to me and handed me a bouquet of flowers with blue carnations.

I'm not advocating being abusive to your parents by any means, but as appropriate, ask the tough questions. You deserve to get answers. But remember to do so respectfully with the understanding that it is a delicate topic and they will most likely not want to discuss it. Respect that and give them time to come around.

There are techniques you can use to gently break down those emotional barriers, such as sending heartfelt cards that express the thoughts you may have trouble communicating. You can send "just because" flowers to your mom, again if appropriate, along with a meaningful heartwarming note or poem. You can reach out and make little efforts to communicate as appropriate to begin chipping away at that proverbial iceberg.

Over time, and with a great deal of effort, my heart changed toward my mother. It changed from the bitterness and hatefulness that I'd covered up for so long to understanding and appreciation. When all is said and done, you are responsible for you life, and it is up to you to take action and do whatever is necessary to make peace with your past.

Be wise and don't consciously follow the non-productive patterns of behavior modeled in your childhood. Learning how to rewrite the software of your mind will help you move beyond your limitations so you can change the printout for your life.

I strongly believe that one of the biggest hindrances to changing your mindset is consuming too much television. If you allow yourself to be socially conditioned, you unconsciously begin to accept unacceptable values and perspectives as your own.

Some people use television to self medicate so they won't have to think about their issues. They can become so absorbed in reality television shows and living vicariously through those characters that they live in a dream-like state about their own life.

I used to be one of those people until one day, when I was in my early twenties, I rushed into my aunt's house asking to watch an episode of a soap opera that was about to come on. My uncle said, "Girl, what you come rushing in here for to watch a television program? Those people getting paid." Then he asked me a profound question: "Do you think those people would rush home to watch you?"

I never quite viewed television the same way again. Not only are the people involved "getting paid," but most of the disempowering and non–life affirming programs, movies, music etc., are a figment of someone's imagination; and too many people accept it as their reality.

Instead, redeem the time wisely by spending those hours on your personal and spiritual development, and watch your life change in the twinkling of an eye.

Transformation begins by shifting from what you used to view, what you used to listen to, and what you used to say out loud to immerse yourself as directed by your Higher Power in the activities that are designed to enhance your life. Also, it's just as important to monitor the self-talk and monkey mind conversations you entertain. Don't entertain them. Capture those disempowering thoughts and bring them into obedience to what you want to create in your Queendom.

If you do this every day, you will get all the clarity you need to move in the direction of your goals and get every desire of your heart fulfilled. The bottom line is you have to adjust your personal self and develop your spiritual self.

I believe people put too much of a burden on "Jesus" to fix it because most people don't want to accept responsibility for their actions or lives. They use "Jesus" as a scapegoat to clean up their chaos, when in fact the Word of God tells us to work out our own salvation.

Many of the hang-ups you have about your traumatic childhood experience stem from constantly thinking about the experience. The work has to be done in the mind. If you keep replaying those old records, you'll remain wounded with unresolved childhood issues.

I believe whenever your soul is ready for a new life lesson, the Universe will always provide a teacher to enlighten you. I believe whatever you need to become healed from negative thought patterns, the Universe will provide at the appointed time. I believe there is nothing impossible for God to do to get you in a state of consciousness of the truth of your being when you open yourself up to believe and receive.

The Slate Wiped Clean

Through a friend, I learned about PSYCH-K®, a process created by founder Rob Williams. I attended the twenty-hour workshop with the expectation of leaving with a renewed mind, free from self-limiting beliefs, and a transformed life. That weekend transformed my life in more ways than I could have imagined.

The workshop location was serene, and the atmosphere was infused with so much dynamic energy, I could sense it was going to be an enlightening weekend. I was a yielded vessel, receptive to whatever the Spirit had in store!

My breakthrough came on the last day of the workshop as I was practicing an exercise with one of the ladies. I was the client, and she was in the role of facilitator. We were wrapping up the session when the instructor walked over to observe us. Based on our feedback about the practice session, the instructor advised us to continue the session because she discerned I had an "unresolved issue with my mother and that I did not love her." Her suggestion was totally unexpected, and I stated to her, "There's no way that I don't love my mom. I love my mother." She smiled and instructed the facilitator to retest me to determine if, subconsciously, I loved my mother. To my surprise, the test revealed I was indeed weak based on that statement. The instructor advised us to continue working until we reconciled that issue.

While working on the "I love my mother" statement, I closed my eyes and saw one hand moving toward another hand that was reaching out to accept a bouquet of flowers. Almost immediately, I noticed a sensation in my heart chakra that at first felt like a pinch. Then I felt lighter as if something that was weighing me down had been lifted off me. I had a very strong sense of relief and peace and then such an overwhelming sensation of authentic joy. Little Shirley was undeniably "happy now," and tears began to flow as if a faucet had been turned on. That opened up a floodgate of joyous laughter and crying at the same time. I was truly crying tears of joy!

The smiling instructor walked over to us again and asked the practice facilitator to test me again for the statement "I love my mother." This time, I passed with flying colors, and I was astonished.

On the drive home, I wondered what Little Shirley would say to Mom now. Because I was energized and vibrating at such a high level, it took a few days for it to subside. About a week later, I made a decision to reach out to her, wondering if I'd be able to connect with her again. I was eager to have another conversation because the first conversation had ended so abruptly, and I felt like something was left unsaid. On the day I decided to have the conversation, I set the intention to be open and ready to receive whatever she wanted to say. Before I could finish my prayer or think of the question to ask, this is what came up from my spirit:

What would the little girl within say to her parents now?

Mom and Dad, in your own subtle ways, you've taught me volumes about life. My heart space is filled with love and respect for you. I hope you forgive me for everything I've done to contribute to your hurt and disappointments. I want you to be proud of me. It's important to me to become a success in life so that your efforts will not have been in vain. I miss you with every fiber of my being and I'll love you forever.

CONCLUSION

My life at times seemed like I was on a roller coaster ride—sometimes speeding through life and other times slowing down with the twists and turns and uphill climbs. Sometimes I'd get to a peak and suddenly drop off into a downward spiral. Through an amazing journey of forgiveness, of healing, and of developing my spiritual self, I am genuinely free from the bondage of my past. That slate has been wiped clean, no residue left behind.

As unbelievable as my journey has been, I have to say I'm feeling pretty darn good about where I am now in regard to my childhood issues. I can honestly say, since that weekend workshop, I have not been bothered by any of those painful childhood memories. I'm at a point where I can remain disconnected from the emotions that were associated with them, and I have no regrets. I have closure on that part of my life.

I am comfortable being my own woman. I love myself for all I'm destined to become, and I am unapologetically living my life in my authentic nature. The adult Shirley is genuinely happy now!

It takes some people a little longer to get where they need to be, but I'm here to tell you that as long as you persevere and follow the music you hear in your heart, you'll get the satisfaction in life you deserve.

This thing called life is serious business and is not for the faint-hearted. The struggles are real, but when you set your course to follow the direction of the God Positioning Satellite inside, you will reach your destination of that place of peace, joy, happiness, and ultimately the affluent life you thought had eluded you.

There will be detours and unexpected stops and traffic jams along the way. So when you're driving through the dark tunnels down the highway of life, keep your high beams on and pay attention to all the signs. No matter how rough the road you're travelling on seems, there are always roads much worse.

If you believe, you will overcome any obstacles that are designed to keep you looking back in the rear view mirror of your life. Don't let them hinder you from pressing on and evolving into the divine person you're meant to be. I would like to share some pearls of wisdom I learned on my journey of transformation. I hope they inspire you to get out of the passenger seat and into the driver's seat of your life, and then make that "You-turn" into the right lane on the highway to your destiny. Namaste!

*If you would like a free downloadable audio version
of the Pearls of Wisdom, email me at
steppingupmygame@aim.com*

ACKNOWLEDGMENTS

I'm honored to have this opportunity to share my story and journey with you. I want to acknowledge and thank you, the reader, for your interest in this topic. I hope this book is as life changing for you as my journey has been for me.

Several people were very supportive of this endeavor and contributed in various ways to encourage me through the completion book.

First, I'd like to start with Ms. Alesha Brown, The Joy Guru, for encouraging me to write my truth unapologetically and for her expert advice and suggestions during the initial stages of developing the story. I'm grateful, Alesha.

My sister, Deborah, I love you dearly. You are the best big sister a person can have. You've been encouraging through the good and bad times. Even when I doubted myself, you believed in me. I thank you so much for sharing your heartfelt story, and I hope you get every desire of your heart. I'll always be grateful for you.

My son, Will, I am so very proud of you. Having you here with me during this journey has truly been a blessing. Every time I shared a small achievement I made writing the book, you beamed with pride. Your pride in me boosted my pride in myself and motivated me to press on. I love you, sweetie, and I'm grateful to have you in my life.

My sons, Quincy and Jared, I'm so proud of you both and grateful for your love and support in all of my endeavors. J, I'm stepping up my game—thanks for the push. I love you both dearly.

My publisher, Tieshena Davis, and her amazing crew, words don't seem adequate to express my gratitude to you for helping to bring my little girl vision to fruition. I am forever grateful.

Namaste!

ABOUT THE AUTHOR

Shirley Williams is a certified life coach and PSYCH-K© facilitator. Her multi-faceted talents meet the needs of women dealing with life issues involving toxic relationships with abusive adult children and others, dealing with low self-esteem, and healing from unresolved childhood issues.

Shirley likes to spend her spare time with family and friends, being outdoors at a park or beach, visiting museums, going to the theatre, traveling, and attending jazz concerts and other live musical events.

To connect, visit her website at
www.shirleytharris.com

REFERENCES

1. "How Childhood Pain Leads to Relationship Trauma in Adulthood." Promises Treatment Center, April 10, 2013. https://www.malibuvista.com/mental-health/how-childhood-pain-leads-to-relationship-trauma-in-adulthood/.

2. Swan, Yol. 2016. "Healing Your Wounded Inner Child. "Soul Guided Coach, February 18. http://soulguidedcoach.com/healing-your-wounded-inner-child/.

3. Collier, Robert. 1947. *Riches Within Your Reach*. New York: TarcherPerigee.

4. Grabbe, Linda, Janell Ball, and Joanne M. Hall. "Girlhood Betrayals of Women Childhood Trauma Survivors in Treatment for Addiction." *Journal of Nursing Scholarship* 48(3).

5. Holmes, Ernest. 2007. *This Thing Called You*. BN Publishing

6. International Center for Reiki Training. "What is Reiki?" Reiki.org. Accessed September 6, 2017. http://www.reiki.org/faq/whatisreiki.html.

7. Bethell, Christina D., Paul Newacheck, Eva Hawes, and Neal Halfon. 2014. "Adverse Childhood Experiences: Assessing The Impact

On Health And School Engagement And The Mitigating Role Of Resilience." *Health Affairs* 33(12): 2106–115. doi: 10.1377/hlthaff.2014.0914.

8. National Center for Injury Prevention and Control, Division of Violence Prevention. 2017. "Child Abuse and Neglect: Risk and Protective Factors." CDC, April 18. https://www.cdc.gov/violenceprevention/childmaltreatment/riskprotectivefactors.html.

RESOURCES AND OTHER INFORMATION

Child Abuse and Neglect: Risk and Protective Factors[1*]

A combination of individual, relational, community, and societal factors contribute to the risk of child abuse and neglect. Although children are not responsible for the harm inflicted upon them, certain characteristics have been found to increase their risk of maltreatment. Risk factors are those characteristics associated with child abuse and neglect—they may or may not be direct causes.

Individual Risk Factors

- Parents' lack of understanding of children's needs, child development, and parenting skills
- Parents' history of child maltreatment in family of origin
- Substance abuse and/or mental health issues including depression in the family
- Parental characteristics such as young age, low education, single parenthood, large number of dependent children, and low income
- Nonbiological, transient caregivers in the home (e.g., mother's male partner)

1* CDC

- Parental thoughts and emotions that tend to support or justify maltreatment behaviors

Family Risk Factors

- Social isolation
- Family disorganization, dissolution, and violence, including intimate partner violence
- Parenting stress, poor parent–child relationships, and negative interactions

Here are other ways your resistance to change and to growing up can manifest in your life:[2]

- Lacking self-discipline to complete a task or project, especially when it's for your own fulfillment
- Dwelling in resentment when things don't go your way
- Feeling powerless and pleasing others to gain some sense of control
- Perceiving yourself like a victim in any way or blaming others for your emotional states
- Expecting people to do what you need or want, as if they owed you something
- Making excuses or justifying yourself, as if you owed them something
- Believing you can heal your wounds *through* others, especially close relationships
- Seeking love and validation outside of yourself

- Following compulsive or addictive behaviors to cope with anxiety, frustration, or stress
- Settling for situations that squelch your independence and joy

Both emotional and spiritual freedom require the maturity that comes from overcoming the obstacles and resistance this archetype projects into your reality.

CREATING DISTINCTIVE BOOKS WITH INTENTIONAL RESULTS

We're a collaborative group of creative masterminds with a mission to produce high-quality books to position you for monumental success in the marketplace.

Our professional team of writers, editors, designers, and marketing strategists work closely together to ensure that every detail of your book is a clear representation of the message in your writing.

Want to know more?
Write to us at info@publishyourgift.com
or call (888) 949-6228

Discover great books, exclusive offers, and more at
www.PublishYourGift.com

Connect with us on social media

@publishyourgift

www.ingramcontent.com/pod-product-compliance
Lightning Source LLC
Chambersburg PA
CBHW071516080526
44588CB00011B/1450